Make Life Matter

BREAK THE EFFECTS OF THE MENTAL PANDEMIC.

Make Life Matter: Break the Effects of the Mental Pandemic by
Matthew L. Wilson

Self published

Queen Creek, AZ

www.MakeLifeMatter.com

For permissions or other inquiries, please contact:
makelifematter.book@gmail.com.

ISBN: 978-0-9892552-4-0

Printed in the USA.

Second Edition

Me: Hey God.

God: Hello.....

Me: I'm falling apart. Can you put me back together?

God: I'd rather not.

Me: Why?

God: Because you aren't a puzzle.

Me: What about all of the pieces of my life falling down?

God: Leave them be, they're supposed to fall off.

Me: You don't understand! I'm breaking down!

God: You're breaking through. You aren't falling apart, you are falling into place. These are growing pains from shedding the things and the people in your life that have been holding you back. Take some deep breaths and allow those pieces to fall off. They were never meant to be a part of you, anyway.

Me: But if I do that, what will be left of me?

God: Only the very best.

Me: I'm scared of changing.

God: My child, you aren't changing, you are becoming.

Me: Becoming who?

God: Becoming who I created you to be! A person of light and love and courage. I made you for more than those shallow pieces with which you are trying to adorn yourself. Let those pieces fall off so you can become who I made you to be.

Me: You mean I'm not broken?

God: No, you're not broken. But you are breaking...like the dawn.

It's a new day, my child.

Become!

Dedication

This book is dedicated to the few who know me better than anyone in the world, yet in spite of my faults, still believe in me:

My dear wife. You have had thousands of reasons to suspend belief in the one who promised you the world 25 years ago. Yet in spite of ongoing evidence to the contrary, you chose to place your faith in the person I was becoming rather than the person I was at the time. Thank you for your undying love, never-ending patience and unwavering belief you have in me to this day. My lifelong commitment is to become the person you have somehow brainwashed yourself into believing I am: Superman. I love you more than you know and hope one day I can grow up to be just like you.

My five children. In spite of my endless supply of lame dad jokes; in spite of the times I impatiently expected you to grow up too fast, you still loved me and somehow gave me one more "I love you, daddy." I'm incredibly proud of who you are all becoming and cannot wait to spoil my grandkids and send them home with you, full of sugar.

One thing you should know about me: I don't believe in any such thing as self made. It has never rang true for me. Everyone is touched by countless thoughts, interruptions, pivots, ideas, inspirations, or nuggets of knowledge that helped them on their journey.

I want to acknowledge many other mentors, most of whom have never met me, but with whom I have a strong connection. Thank you for the influence you may never know you have had on me.

My parents (both sets)

Napoleon Hill

Og Mandino

Dr. Joe Dispenza

James Allen

Brooke Castillo

Lewis Howes

Solomon Sampson

Bob Proctor

Tony Robbins

Grant Cardone

Eckhart Tolle

James Clear

Brendan Broschard

Gary Vaynerchuk

Jim Rohn

John Maxwell

Hal Elrod

Dr. Daniel Amen

Norman Vincent Peale

Eric & Kim Valdez

John & Kim Kight

Barry Clarkson & Equis Leadership

Jason & Crystal Patello

Jim Kwik

John Waters

And so many more!

And, of course, all the glory, thanks and praise to a loving Heavenly Father who has seen fit to bless me in my life through all the ups and downs. I owe everything to the One who has given me everything.

Table of Contents

INTRODUCTION 1

CHAPTER 1: PROTECT YOUR MIND 7

CHAPTER 2: WHAT IN THE CELL ARE YOU MADE OF? 27

CHAPTER 3: WHY YOUR BRAIN MATTERS 53

CHAPTER 4: BRAIN VS. MIND 73

CHAPTER 5: DO YOU MIND? 89

CHAPTER 6: FROM THOUGHTS TO RESULTS 107

CHAPTER 7: YOUR IDENTITY CONTINUUM 133

CHAPTER 8: THE VOICES IN YOUR HEAD 157

CHAPTER 9: 12 STEPS TO MAKE YOUR LIFE MATTER 183

Introduction

Call it Murphy's Law, or just bad luck but one truth in life is that the faster and harder you move, the more friction you can expect. In fact, the most inspiring stories we hear on a TEDx stage are those who have suffered the most from the worst life has thrown at them. And they stand up again, shoulders back, head held high. After all, who is inspired by the story of the guy who glided up the escalator to the top of the mountain of success? There's a TED talk that never got any views.

Life is not a matter of avoiding risk because that doesn't exist. Life is about which risks you choose and how you handle them when they arise. Get out of bed and you've already taken on risk. What if you pull your back out getting dressed? Or jam your gums while brushing your teeth? Heading for work, you could trip and fall down your front porch steps, get hit by a car or even worse, get pooped on by a pigeon. Tiptoeing safely to your death is no way to live your life. There's nothing inspiring about playing small and quiet. Life is about pressing forward firmly in the face of the storm and getting back up each time you fall over.

The first time you took a step, you fell down. You accepted risk as a natural and inseparable part of life. And then you grew up and you learned to avoid risk and be afraid of it. A professional skydiver doesn't think twice about jumping out of a perfectly good airplane. The average Joe would rather die a thousand deaths.

The difference lies in what your brain has become accustomed to through thoughts, beliefs and actions. The risk is there either way, it always has been.

You might try to eliminate risk by bubble wrapping yourself safely in your bedroom. But even then, you still risk suffocating. Risk is an everyday and inescapable part of life. That's why there's such a thing as insurance. You can take out an insurance policy for nearly anything and everything. There's even a carrier in Florida offering alien abduction insurance. And rumor has it, they've even paid out on a claim.

As a life insurance agent, I have a very meaningful line of work. I get to protect people against things like death, cancer and horrific car accidents. You never know which day is the day something horrific could happen. When that day comes, you need to already have a policy in force. You don't go looking for a life insurance policy right after you find out you have terminal cancer. Like your body, your mind is exposed to risk every day but it's a different kind of risk. Every day, billions are spent to capture your attention. And just like life insurance, you need to have your mindset right before the challenges arise.

This book is about risk, your mind, and what you can do about it. It's unlike any other book you have ever picked up. You'll notice coloring pages and a host of free tools on **MakeLifeMatter.com** you can use to help you. As you read, keep pens and highlighters handy. Mark up passages that mean something and cross off parts that don't. But pay the closest attention to new thoughts and ideas that come into your mind and heart as a result of reading this book. Things completely unrelated to what's written in ink. Those are nuggets from God directly for your life. They come as a fringe benefit of you making the effort to read and enhance your mind.

Your mind is the biggest marvel in the universe. Some days, it's your worst enemy, other days it's your most remarkable asset. Mine it and you'll unleash incredible potential. Let's make your life matter...starting on the inside.

Feel free to tear this sheet out
and color it as you listen to the
audio, available at:
www.MakeLifeMatter.com

Inspire others by posting finished
coloring pages with hashtag:
#MakeLifeMatter.

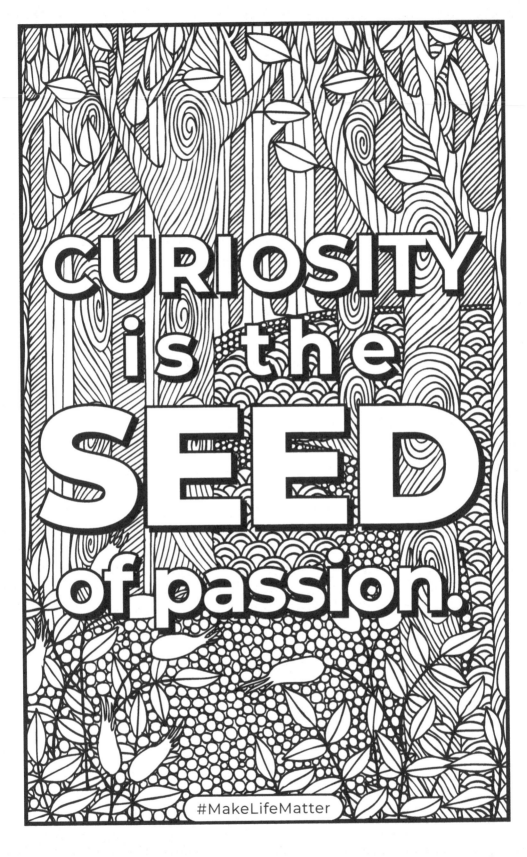

CHAPTER 1
Protect Your Mind

You're driving along in backwoods, small-town America. You finally admit you're a little lost as your mom's voice echoes in your head, "please don't forget to bring a map." Around the next bend, you enter a quaint town, with a curious sign:

WELCOME TO THOUGHTINGHAM

Thoughtingham? The town feels strangely familiar, although you don't recall having been here before. Instinctively, you slow down because you know how cops are in small towns. But there's something different about Thoughtingham. Something is not right. You chuckle uncomfortably as you pass by a run-down home with a yard full of locals in the middle of a food fight. Hmm...that's odd. It reminds you of that time in third grade... SCREEECH! Suddenly, you slam on your breaks, nearly hitting two kids chasing each other across the street. But that's just the beginning. As you drive into town, you can't help but notice there's something not right about this place.

People are everywhere, doing whatever they please. Old ladies are shoplifting, teenagers are speeding and children are breaking windows. Traffic lights are nothing more than suggestions. The streets are full of drivers who should never have been given a license in the first place. Old folks in wheelchairs are racing through traffic and causing accidents. Toddlers are running around, tagging parked cars with profane messages that would make a sailor blush.

Nobody in Thoughtingham seems to care about anything!

Your grip tightens around your steering wheel as your focus returns to your driving, this time more intense. You swerve to avoid a collision. White knuckled, you glide carefully through the main drag, passing by the city hall, a park, an abandoned library, the sheriff's office...

Ah, the sheriff's office!

Without thinking, you pull into the parking lot, hop out and march up to the front door. You may be an outsider, but you have to know why law enforcement would turn a blind eye to the entire town.

Your heart skips a beat as you walk in. Part of you says it's not your business. Another part argues that you have a moral responsibility to report a crime. Or 1,000 of them. You're greeted by an older lady dressed in beige. She has a deep voice, short hair, and glasses. She taps away rhythmically at her keyboard as you wonder if she even noticed you. Does she ever get out of her chair? How many days old is that coffee?

"Good morning," you announce, hoping for some acknowledgment.

The pause is long enough to make anyone uncomfortable. The lady finishes typing her sentence and glances up.

"I suppose. Can I help you?"

"Yeah, is the sheriff here?"

"Always," comes the reply. "He lives in his office."

The sheriff must have overheard. "Hello, friend. Welcome to our town!"

"Hi, thanks. Um, I don't know if you've noticed but would you look outside?"

The sheriff pauses, a little confused. "Anything in particular?"

"Pick something! I mean, look: there's a kid on a pogo stick...in traffic!"

"Oh him? That's just Joey. He won't hurt you."

Suddenly, a jarring splat nearly broke the window. You look over to see tomato guts oozing down the glass.

"We'll just clean that up later," the sheriff chuckles. "Now, what's your concern?"

You're at a loss for words. But you seem to find some anyway. "You are the sheriff, right? Everyone's breaking the law- it's crazy out there. You can't just let them..."

"Oh, they're just having fun," the sheriff interrupts. "Besides, they've always been this way. I tried one time to change them, but it didn't work. So, now we just go along with it. Right, Fran?"

The old lady nods as she returns diligently to her typing.

"Anyway," the sheriff continues, "we're always glad to have visitors. Would you like a map of the area? How long will you be staying with us?"

THERE'S A NEW SHERIFF IN TOWN

The town of Thoughtingham exists in the minds of billions of humans all over the world. In fact, its population is greater than all the world's major cities combined. And there's a sheriff in each one. Unless that sheriff does his job, your thoughts run around breaking the law all day, every day. Unsupervised, unchecked, and unquestioned.

But what if the Attorney General came to town and took over the sheriff's place? How long would it take to "clean up the place?" A group of thoughts goes to trial. A few others need to be detained. Many are simply banished from the kingdom without a hearing. It would take some work, but over time, the citizens of Thoughtingham would begin to notice that there is a "new norm." And a beautiful thing would happen: everyone would begin to follow the rules.

This is what's going on inside each of our minds every day. It's why so many of us never seem to make any credible progress in our lives. One lazy sheriff will never change an entire town of unruly people. Even as the top authority, his power is useless because it is not recognized or respected. But what if the Attorney General took over?

"Judge, may I approach the bench?"

"OK, thought, but make it quick."

"Judge, I've been around forever. I am accepted all throughout this town. Besides, look at all the evidence to support that I am true! I propose that..."

"Overruled!"

"Wait, what? You didn't even..."

"Overruled. You may be seated."

"But your Honor. With all due respect, I think you should hear me out."

"For the last time, overruled. If I have to say it again, I'll slap you with contempt and have you escorted out of the courtroom."

Here's a principle you can hang your hat on: the criminals in your mind will always resist the law. Not only will they try to get away with as much as they can but they will also revert back to how things were if ever the sheriff begins to relax on his duties. Your mind is pre-wired to do what it's always done. To bring about any significant change will require a consistent, focused effort from an Attorney General figure named Conscious. He's the highest-ranking mental law-enforcement officer. He's in charge of everyone, including your sheriff.

Provided you bring him out of hiding.

Every day, more than 50,000 thoughts bounce around inside your mind like balls in a pinball machine. Some of them are true, some are half-truths and others are bald-faced lies. We will learn later that whether or not they are true is not as relevant as you think. But ultimately, it's up to you to detain and question each one of them, determine whether or not they're honorable citizens of your society, then take any necessary legal action to ensure they adhere to the law. It's a big job but someone's gotta do it.

That someone is you. You are the one in the driver's seat. It's you who wears the law enforcement badge on your chest. But in order to make any significant change, you have to get to the root of the problem: your perception.

The problem with your problems is that you think your problem is the problem. It's not. The problem is what you make your problem mean by how you think about your problem. That's the problem.

Read that again slowly, I promise it will make sense.

Suppose you leave a job because the boss sucks, the job is too hard or you're not being paid enough. Perhaps you have not learned this lesson yet. The consequence is you get to bring your mindset (the problem) with you to the next job. And it's only a matter of time before the problem (your thought pattern) rears its ugly head again and you're looking for the next "solution" somewhere outside of you (and it's still not there). Rinse and repeat. The solution is *inside* you, my friends. Not outside. The grass is not always greener on the other side of the fence. The grass is greener where it's watered.

YOUR HIGHER NETWORK

If you're a student of success, you have likely heard the phrase, "your network is your net worth." There's even a book written with that title. Businessmen and women have found a lot of truth to the idea- who you know can be more valuable than what you know. So, let's take a look at your network. If I were to ask you what your network looks like, how would you answer? What types of connections do you have? Where would you go to find the answer?

Networking can be a dirty word. The first thing that may come to mind is an awkward event where a collection of business people gather together for the purpose of establishing new connections. You might think of networking as a bunch of Type A personalities competing for who can go back to their office with the largest stack of prospective leads. But let's look beyond the stereotype. Your network also includes your social media channels and your database of contacts. What about your non-business networks such as your friends at the gym, library, grocery store, or dog park. If you were to sit down and take the time, you'd likely be amazed at how extensive your network is.

But let's take it one step further. Have you considered your neural network? If there is any truth behind the idea that your network is your net worth, imagine the value of a network with 100 trillion connections. The largest LinkedIn network has approximately 16 million connections, a minuscule fraction of the network you carry inside your own mind everywhere you go.

Your neural network is built primarily by others who have influenced your mind in ways unbeknownst to you. In fact, the whole idea that someone is "self-made" is simply not true. Nobody can claim they made it 100% on their own. It's literally impossible. Even those with the most remarkable rags to riches stories have an uncle, coach, teacher, parent, neighbor, or even an author of a book who has taught, influenced, or otherwise enhanced the life or mindset of that person in some way. What about the gifts given by God? Claiming to be self-made is a narrow-minded mentality, not to mention a lack of gratitude for how others have helped you along your way. Often, intangible influence is much more significant than the amount of accumulated financial resources (the barometer society uses to define a self-made person).

Your brain's capacity to learn, memorize, solve problems and retain information is unlimited. As of the time of this writing, no human being has ever reportedly filled up her brain and reached the limit. I doubt anyone has even come close. So the question is: how can you leverage a network like that to help your net worth? How can you get those little neurons buzzing around the room, handing out business cards?

THE ULTIMATE GENIE WISH

What if genies were real? What if you picked up a lamp at a garage sale somewhere, rubbed it and a genie actually came out. He has some bad news, though. He's been used a lot over the years and he's down to just one single wish left. Not three like everyone else, just one. What would you wish for? It's an easy solution- you'd wish for unlimited wishes. Now, that's working the system, right?

A narrow-minded person might point out that you had one wish and you got nothing in return, only more wishes. But you see the long-term value. You understand that you gave up one wish in the short term to gain an infinite number more. Good trade, right? The goose has laid a golden egg.

I just described learning. If there's one superpower you could give yourself, it would be the capacity to learn anything. Because once you get good at that, you can learn to become or attain whatever you want in life. But you have to be willing to go through the process of learning to learn first. You have to give up that first wish in order to get the rest of them.

And are you ready for some good news? This is a superpower you already possess. It's not fantasy. You already have the capacity to learn. God gave that to you. Wasn't that thoughtful of Him? You can learn new things up until the day you die. Even new ways of thinking.

Some of the best advice I can give to anyone is this: learn to love to learn.

At your disposal, you have what world-renowned scientists agree is the most powerful supercomputer in the world. It's 100% yours and you have full access to it every day, as much as you want. The biggest tragedy in life is falling short of discovering your potential. Most people on their deathbeds have more regrets about what they DIDN'T do than what they did. The human spirit craves discovering our limits. It's how we're wired.

You may have heard that you use only about 10% of your brain. It's not true. You use 100% of your brain, just in different ways. It's not how MUCH your brain you use that matters, it's HOW you use your brain. There's a lot of misinformation floating around out there. Before accepting anything as truth, employ your sheriff, detain the thought and do your homework. Only grant citizenship in Thoughtingham if it is true and serves you well. And certainly don't pass along a thought that will limit, hurt or belittle others.

In school, you study hard, read, repeat, memorize and

spend a weekend cramming for a test. You flood your brain with the information you need just long enough that it doesn't leak out the trap door in the back of your head before you're able to pass the test. You learned that mistakes are bad and asking questions is embarrassing and even shameful. A large part of what you learned in school wasn't from a textbook at all, or even in a classroom. Some of the most impactful learning has to do with how you think, interact, and other habits. It comes from teachers, fellow classmates, and others around you. No matter how hard you may try, you cannot NOT learn. It's a matter of what and how deeply.

The most valuable thing you can learn at school is a love for learning itself because life's greatest lessons come after you graduate from school. HOW to learn and WHY to learn are infinitely more important than WHAT to learn. You'll always be a student but you won't always be in the classroom.

Have you tried to help one of your kids with homework? Remember the popular show, "Are you Smarter Than a Fifth Grader?" Why don't you remember all the answers? Didn't you graduate from High School? It proves how easily you forget when you don't truly learn the material.

Your brain can learn by memorizing content, but it learns best when you teach it to others. If you want to learn and retain the principles in this book, start teaching someone else what you learn— maybe a spouse, co-worker, even your child. The act of teaching solidifies the concepts in your mind and significantly increases your chances of remembering the concepts later on down the road. Most people do not understand the full potential of their minds.

In order to move forward, you might have to clear out some space. Some of what you learned early in life will need to be UNlearned: habits, behaviors, "facts" and methods commonly accepted by the collective cultural subconscious. This is not as easy to do as you may think because you have accepted them into your belief system, which means it runs deep. Many of these ideas have been there long enough that you simply accept them as truth. Your truth. They feel true because they're familiar to you, like a good friend. They've spent years in your mind, unquestioned. But that doesn't make them true.

Until you're willing to be wrong about your core beliefs, who you can become will always be limited. So, read, question, absorb and learn with insatiable curiosity. Get obsessed with learning. Become a shorter of truths and insights and a collector of crazy thoughts and ideas. When you discover something worth passing on, something you want to truly internalize, teach it to someone else. It blesses their life and yours in return.

Let's dive in now to the greatest superpower this world has ever known. Not something out of a comic book- we're talking about real life. Your life.

GET TO THE SOURCE

Suppose you are enjoying a nice evening, reading in your favorite chair. From a distance, you hear the most beautiful sound in the world: your children happily doing the dishes. Suddenly, one of your kids interrupts this peaceful scene running frantically into the room. It's the youngest with an urgent message.

"The kitchen is flooding!"

You put your book down and run in to see the tap running full blast. The sink is clogged up and water is spewing over the counter onto the floor.

At the scene of the crime is your oldest child who is doing his best to get everything under control. Using a rag, he is on a cycle, soaking up the water on the ground and wringing out the rag into the sink again.

Over and over.

"Don't worry, mom! I got this."

The problem is obvious. It's not the growing puddle on the floor, although that much water on a kitchen floor is always a problem. The real problem is the source of the water. Unless you turn off the faucet, you will never get rid of the puddle no matter how many rags you use to mop it up. The one feeds the other.

From your perspective, the solution is both obvious and simple. But it's not so obvious to your little kids. They're right in the thick of the chaos. Fortunately, they're young and innocent so it's still kind of cute. Now, if your college student struggled to figure it out, not so cute.

Either way, the lesson is obvious: you might be the water-mopping champion of your high school but even mad skills like those will not dry out the floor. As long as you only treat the symptom, the problem will never go away. You HAVE to fix the source.

One of the messages my kids will tell you I'm famous for is that you cannot ignore your problems. An ignored problem does not go away on its own. It will find friends and come back stronger and move in until it cannot be ignored any longer and creates a much larger problem. Learn to handle problems early on while they're small. Before you have to remodel your entire kitchen.

MIND INSURANCE

Have you ever felt like you're living life in a loop? Do you find yourself repeating the same types of behaviors, habits, patterns, and results in your life? Do you keep falling back into the same you as last year? You're spending all your time mopping and what you need is to first turn off the faucet.

Thank goodness your kitchen is insured. But what about your mind? What insurance policy protects your mind? There's not an insurance carrier in the world that does that. It doesn't exist...outside of you. But it does exist inside of you. And it's not only your responsibility but it's also a privilege uniquely reserved for you and you alone. It simply cannot be delegated to another.

Your mind is the single most valuable asset in the world. And the world is happy to tell you all about it in fun, catchy phrases that get tossed around like hot potatoes. Instagram is full of inspirational memes, "the mind is a terrible thing to waste," and "change your mind and you change your life." And while they're true, what do you do with them? Share, like, and comment? What do they truly mean to you, outside of just another clever thing to say? Press pause on the world and turn your attention inward.

Most life insurance policies come with an immediate benefit because people want that. You sign a document, it gets approved and bingo, you're insured, full benefit from day one. Plus double payout if you die by accident, and a waiver of premium rider to boot! We love our instant gratification.

But a mind insurance policy doesn't work like that. It can be underwritten and instantly approved by you at any time. There is no age requirement, no application, or extra questionnaires to fill out. There are no medications to report or illnesses to navigate. What's more, even the poorest people in the world can afford one. The currency used to pay the premiums is awareness.

And the best part: this policy is yours for the taking any time you like. It's as if God Himself said, "This one's on the house."

But insuring your mind is not a cakewalk. The most valuable policy in the world doesn't come easy. You have to build it up one conscious change at a time. No amount of money can purchase this policy. It comes with no guarantees. There is no cash value or fancy riders to enhance the policy. No cash back option or living benefits to help cover a critical, chronic or terminal illness. Your mind insurance policy cannot cover children, spouses, or other loved ones (although it can affect them in a positive way). It's a single policy created and designed, by the owner, for the owner. Everyone is responsible for his own policy.

Life insurance companies are on the hook every year for billions of dollars in death claims. When you protect your mind, the benefits far outweigh even the most substantial monetary payout a life insurance policy would ever deliver. Benefits include peace, joy, confidence, faith, positivity, healing, strength, fulfillment, achievement, growth, and mini-miracles along the way.

Doesn't that sound like a more peaceful Thoughtingham?

*Feel free to tear this sheet out
and color it as you listen to the
audio, available at:*
www.MakeLifeMatter.com

*Inspire others by posting finished
coloring pages with hashtag:*
#MakeLifeMatter.

CHAPTER 2
What in the CELL Are You Made of?

Significant progress has been made in the last 50 years about our understanding of how the brain works. The good news is we no longer have to guess about what's going on. Today, we KNOW. Modern medical imaging equipment, scans, and other types of tests allow us to take a peek deep inside the biology of our brains to understand how the wiring and circuitry happen.

But knowledge alone does nothing for you. What do you do with that knowledge? You must take action. Two people can walk out of the same motivational seminar. One is inspired, puts the information into practice and his life is changed forever. The other can't leave soon enough and remembers it as sixty minutes he'll never get back. Same information, same lecture. Two different reactions, two different mindsets.

Once you understand the miracle of who you are, you will begin to think and act differently. Your confidence will increase. You'll stop worrying about other people's opinions. You'll have added strength to face fear, cross chasms of doubt and willingly step out into the unknown with faith. The transformation begins with a deep-rooted understanding of what a freaking miracle you really are. You no longer base your worth on height, weight, skin color, genes, income, health conditions...

any of it. Nothing could ever diminish your value.

The more I learn about the human body, the more I come to understand that every person I meet is literally a physical miracle! Here are just a few things that go on inside you every day, non-stop without you even knowing. Check this out:

Your body is made of approximately 7 octillion atoms (that's 7,000,000,000,000,000,000,000,000,000 atoms). I'd hate to be the guy who was tasked to count them all and verify that.

- Your nostrils take turns with the breathing workload. Chivalry is not dead! I can just hear them, "Why don't you go first." "No, no, let me help you- I insist." As two holes on the same appendage, they've learned to work together.

- Speaking of your nose, it can differentiate between 1 trillion different smells. A trillion! That's a thousand billion.

- Your mouth makes about a half quart of spit every day. Gross right? I don't know what you'd do with a half quart of spit. I'm sure we could think of something but let's not.

- You regenerate all your stomach cells every five days! This makes sense because the acid in your stomach can eat metal. So I'm sure cells don't have a chance to live longer than five days, anyway.

- Your heart beats 100,000 times a day, pumping enough blood to fill four Olympic-sized swimming pools by the end of your life.

- If you removed all of your blood vessels and stretched them out end to end, it would wrap around the earth's equator four times. Plus, you would die.

- You don't technically hear with your ears. You hear with your brain. Your ears merely gather the information and provide it for your brain to interpret...if it wants to. So the next time someone says, "You only hear what you want to hear," you can wholeheartedly agree. We all do. The same thing with your sight- your eyes deliver the information; your brain does the seeing.

- Your skin's outer layer sheds every two to four weeks. So if it's been at least a month since you've seen a friend, you should greet her with, "Who are you? I've never seen you before."

- Your body can (and does) heal itself. Doctors cannot heal you. Hospitals and fancy state-of-the-art equipment cannot heal you. All they can do is create an environment where your body (and mind) can heal itself. That's how awesome you are!

As you can see, it's quite a miracle that you live and breathe and do what you do. Let's take it a level or two deeper. Your body is made up of cells, which are made of molecules that are made of atoms. And what is an atom made of? An atom is 99.9999% energy and .00001% subatomic particles (protons, neutrons, and a nucleus). So you're overwhelmingly made up of empty space filled with waves of energy (although some mornings it doesn't feel like it). The part of you that is physical matter is such a small percentage of what makes up your being that it almost doesn't even matter. It's the non-matter (energy) that matters most. Why then do so many of us judge ourselves based on our physical appearance? Good question, we'll dive into that later.

YOUR BRAIN IS PLASTIC

No, that's not me being rude. It's true. Not literally, but in more ways than you think. Neuroplasticity was first discovered around 1948 and became popular a decade or so later, as the concept took root and technology evolved. Basically, it refers to your brain's ability to adjust, adapt and change physiologically as a result of your thinking. It does this by forming new neural pathways in response to new thoughts and thought patterns. It's your brain's ability to be plastic.

Your brain is malleable. This is why when you make a decision we call it "making up your mind." Every time you think a new thought, a new neural pathway is formed in your brain, otherwise known as a synaptic connection. It's a physical reaction to a non-physical event. And the more you think that thought (or others like it), the more neural pathways are formed to support it and that thought becomes a habit or your new default way of thinking. Similar thought patterns are then able to come easier and more naturally, eventually transforming your entire mindset. In other words, neurons that wire together fire together.

Your grandpa probably taught you that "Practice makes perfect." But did you realize that also applies to your thoughts? In other words, the more you think a certain way, the more you reinforce that way of thinking. It is within your ability to reprogram your mind any way you like at any time you like. It doesn't matter how old you are, your brain is subject to change. No restrictions apply. Batteries not required. Available in all states.

The dangerous part of this is you are subject to influence by everyone and everything around you all day long. Whether you're purposely programming your mind or not, it's constantly being programmed by something or someone. Whether you agree with the idea or not is completely irrelevant. Your subconscious mind will be programmed by your internal and external environments. It cannot pick and choose from whom or what it will be influenced. This is why you need your conscious mind to get the job done.

One of the most important jobs your sheriff has is to scrutinize what thoughts he allows in. He's your gatekeeper. If a thought doesn't pass Thoughtingham's standards, do not let the thought enter. And if one slips in through that little hole near the back gate, arrest it and escort it out. Word will get around- Thoughtingham has a new way of doing things. Any and all thoughts of fear, shame, limited self-beliefs, and doubt are no longer welcome in your town.

Develop a zero-tolerance rule for negativity and gossip. Surround yourself with people, places, and environments that support the way of thinking that will serve you and align with your vision and goals. Your mind is the number one single most precious asset you own. Guard it like the hope diamond.

YOUR BRAIN IS A PHARMACY

When you're physically sick, what do you do? You visit a doctor. And what does your doctor do? She checks you out, makes a diagnosis, and writes a prescription. You take the prescription to a pharmacy where you get medicine that is supposed to help your body get better. Hopefully, the medicine is temporary and you can return to your normal state.

However, many of us have become *dependent* on the medicine prescribed by our doctor, without exploring alternative methods of solving the problem. Granted, anyone who puts themselves through that much education has earned my respect. But in my time as a life insurance agent, I have observed first-hand the costly effects of an ongoing prescription that treats a symptom but ignores the source of the problem, sometimes requiring additional medications to counter the side effects of the first. The dependent patient goes back year after year for refills while the ailment remains unresolved.

Granted, there's certainly a place for medicine, but do not underestimate the healing power you already contain within yourself.

What about emotional illness? Where do you go when your body needs to be happier or your mood needs elevating? Where do you go for that kind of medicine? Your internal pharmacy.

The world's most powerful pharmacy is located in your head. Your brain is made up of 100 billion neurons, or brain cells. These neurons make and release chemical signals (called neurotransmitters) to other cells throughout the brain and down into your body. Those signals have an enormous impact on your mood and your emotions. Think of microscopic radio towers sending messages on how your body should feel about certain things. You have many different neurotransmitters, some of which haven't been discovered or understood yet. Here are four of the more common ones in your brain:

Endorphins are the feel-good chemicals that mask any pain you're going through and boost pleasure. Think of an opioid prescription for severe back pain. If you're emotionally distraught, you could use a hit of endorphins to elevate your mood. You can release this chemical through exercise. Other ways to induce endorphins include having sex, meditating, and laughing.

Oxytocin is the warm, fuzzy chemical that makes you feel trusted, cozy, and loved. Your body produces this chemical when you do things like wrestle around on soft grass with a litter of adorable puppies. It's been nicknamed the "cuddle hormone."

Dopamine is the reward or "good news" chemical. It's the feeling that you get when you know you're going to succeed at something. When your expectation for a reward is elevated, dopamine is the chemical that caused it. And when you achieve a goal, dopamine is released as a reward for a job well done. Your body releases this chemical when you serve others and when you have loving thoughts. It's also induced through exercise, which seems to be the remedy for nearly every ailment known to mankind. Dopamine is the addictive hit you crave that drives you to check an email or social media notification.

Serotonin is the "I'm important" chemical. It's an antidepressant that can boost your confidence in yourself. When this chemical is released from your brain you get the feeling that you are important, helping you feel happy. You get this chemical from being outside in the sunlight and also from exercising and having happy, positive thoughts. It can also be released when you challenge yourself and achieve new limits. It's also associated with memory and learning.

If you want to study this in more depth, Dr. Joe Dispenza is a master at linking the power of the mind and body. He backs up all his work with scientific data and has helped hundreds of people like you learn to harness the power of the mind to heal ailments of the body.

Dr. Dispenza teaches that you already have the chemistry you need to heal yourself, you simply need to learn how to tap into those resources.

EXTRA, EXTRA, DON'T READ ALL ABOUT IT

Now that we have a basic understanding of what's going on inside your head (brain and mind), let's consider one of the most powerful messaging networks ever invented: the news media. Major media outlets spend bucket loads of money on high-paying salaries for some of the world's most gifted and educated copywriters to write headlines that make you want to click on the link. When exposed, you hardly stand a chance against those kinds of forces.

Your precious mind is exposed to it in mass every single day. The forces are so great, to overcome it requires a significant amount of intentional effort. In fact, proper thinking is likely the hardest work you will ever do in your life. It's no wonder so many people today have anxiety and other mental health disorders.

Do you know what the news media does best? It finds things that you didn't know you needed to worry about and convinces you that you now need to worry about them. Think about that. The story of racism. The child molester. The drug bust. The officer shooting. The kidnapping. The list goes on and on. Before you knew about the story, your day was going fine. But once you've exposed your mind to it, emotions enter the scene. Now you're upset, bothered, heated, enraged, or filled with hate you didn't have before. And with prolonged exposure, you become a calloused, crusty shell of a person, gunkified by thoughts of negativity, anger, and bitterness.

You may have noticed when scrolling through the news, the headline itself does not usually represent an accurate depiction of the entire story. Sometimes it's completely misleading because the headline's job is not to give you the story. The headline's job is to appeal to your subconscious mind and suck you in, increasing the media's ratings one click at a time. It's called clickbait. Keyboard warriors feast on a diet of headlines, further perpetuating a collective mindset of fear. The attention > curiosity > dopamine hit cycle literally becomes an addiction.

Why do so many feel such an obligation to keep up with what's going on in the world when they have difficulty keeping up with their own lives? It's such a big place- how can you keep up with it all? More importantly, what benefit do you get out of it? Is this what God designed you to do with your life?

Your life will be better for NOT knowing the negative news stories. Just because technology has given you access to the world, doesn't mean you should take advantage of it. Before the internet, there were newsworthy stories happening all over the world you never knew about. Today, those same stories exist, only now you get exposed to them. And with a single click, you can follow them from the moment you wake up to the moment you fall asleep. With your permission, it comes flooding into your home through televisions, radios, phones, iPads, computers, and other devices. It's no wonder depression and suicide levels continue to rise. The world's always been a negative place. It's also always been a positive place. Which feed are you allowing into your brain?

One thing I know about you is your brain loves negative news. You may even be addicted to it. I know this because you're a human and it's human nature to crave negativity. CNN doesn't get high ratings running a feel-good story about a man who helped a stranded stranger on the side of the road. The news is overwhelmingly negative because that's what sells, not because that's how the world is. Yet, if left unchecked, your subconscious mind picks up the narrative that the world's going to hell in a handbasket.

Media companies spend millions upon millions to attract your attention. And they'll do it any way they can. They know they don't make a penny unless they have an audience. They want you to let them into your precious town and lock up the sheriff. They even offer their own law enforcement services free of charge, which sounds like a good deal on the surface. Just join a newsletter, like, comment, or subscribe and the headlines will begin to pour in automatically without any effort on your part. Tools to help make life convenient for you. But in the end, you become the tool that was played.

ALGORITHM ADDICTION

Social media sites are programmed to figure out what you like and feed you more of it. Every click you make, every time you pause on a message, every time you comment, like, or share, it's all tracked. With every interaction, you're teaching an algorithm more about you. You're slowly building an artificial intelligence clone of yourself. It's all recorded into a database nearly as powerful as your mind. Only this machine has a photographic memory and the stickiness of a barnacle on a ship. Besides the news, your mind is exposed to 5,000 or more marketing messages every single day. Major tech companies hire the most brilliant gurus in the world to attract and influence that small piece of real estate in your head. That's how precious your mind is. And everyone wants a piece of it.

Isn't it interesting that social media sites call it a "feed?" That's exactly what you're doing to your mind: feeding it an all-you-can-eat buffet of high fructose corn syrup. What you eat becomes part of you. Political pundits and major news anchors use their feeds to serve up misinformation and opinions, not facts. What once was a neutral topic has become politically charged and skewed. What's left to believe? How can you tell what is what? Even the so-called facts can be altered to fit an agenda.

You don't have to do much in order for the unruly thought citizens to find you like a heat-seeking missile.

The only thing required for a field to grow weeds is for the farmer to do nothing. Yet a beautiful garden requires proactive and intentional work every single day: watering, weeding, fertilizing, and caring for the garden. Mindset is not a checklist item- you're never done working on it. Protecting your mind is an ongoing, lifelong commitment because weeds start growing the moment you stop preventing them.

The good news is there is good news everywhere- you just have to subscribe to it. Just as your feed has learned to serve up negativity, you can also program it to serve up positivity. Start by unliking, unfriending, and unfollowing anything that does not enhance your life in some way. Unsubscribe your way to a healthier mindset.

Click the switch inside your mind to subscribe to a new way of thinking or looking at the world. Maybe an airplane crashed, but think of all the airplanes that landed safely today without a single death or injury. Of course, there was a fatal accident, but consider how many dads made it home safely to their families tonight after work. Unemployment may be up, but what about all those who just started a new job? Somewhere, somebody is planning a vacation they've been dreaming of all their lives. Someone is building a well to help a thirsty village in Africa. Others are retiring early, conquering cancer, and finding the love of their lives.

None of these stories made the headlines at CNN. But they can make headlines over at MNN (mental news network). So if the news is not broadcasting these messages, you might have to broadcast them to yourself by simply paying attention. The world is a beautiful place. Are you seeing it? Your mind is a news station. What are you broadcasting?

NOBODY ELSE HAS ONE LIKE YOURS

If I were to ask you to think of a symbol that represents how unique you are, what do you think of? Most people would say your fingerprint because it is 100% unique. It's why they like to store them in FBI databases. They can use a fingerprint to determine with accuracy the identity of a person.

But did you know your brain has its own unique brainprint? Brains are not so easy to stamp onto a piece of paper, so we go with the thumbs. But your brain is 100% unique to you and you can know with certainty there is nobody in the entire world with one exactly the same as yours. Just as no two journeys through life are the same, no two brains are the same. In fact, no two brains are the same because no two journeys are the same.

Your brain has been wired by thoughts, beliefs, labels, habits, patterns, and cultural norms from every environment of your life since you were born. Your genes, your family upbringing, your customs and cultures, your family traditions, your friends, teachers- all of it has formed your lens through which you see the world, resulting in your very own unique brainprint. Every influence, no matter how small, has made its mark on you.

Like a pair of glasses, your mind is your prescription lens through which you see the world. It can be difficult to understand someone else's point of view (what they see through their lenses) because you are so accustomed to yours. Looking through a pair of another person's prescription glasses, you might wonder, "How can you even see anything through these?!" In reality, it's the only way they can see anything clearly. When it comes to glasses, everyone understands. So why can it be such a challenge for so many of us to see through the lens of other people's minds? Seeing from another's perspective can save or change relationships.

Someone with green-tinted lenses sees everything green. Another person wearing blue-tinted lenses sees the world in blue. Both can (and do) argue all day long about how much the other is wrong. But who is right? Neither of them- it's how they perceive the world that means everything. How they perceive it does not make it that way in real life. Our perception truly becomes our reality. As Ed Harris famously says in the Truman Show, "We accept the reality of the world with which we're presented. It's as simple as that."

How you see things is everything. It makes all the difference. External to us are circumstances, which are neutral. It's we who make them good or bad. Someone can come from a drug-infested, abusive, poverty-stricken childhood and use that to tell an inspiring story of overcoming and achievement. He chooses to be grateful for his upbringing because he sees it as the very thing that made him strong, gave him drive and helped him know early in life exactly what he DIDN'T want. He wouldn't trade his childhood for anything.

Another person may come from that same challenging background and yet she sees it as the curse of her lifetime. She blames it for all her failures and manifests more of the same through thought habits that keep her entrenched in the very mire she loathes. Same circumstances, completely different outcomes. What's the difference? Perspective. It's you, the meaning maker, who gets to decide whether your circumstances are good, bad or indifferent. Change how you see things and you'll give them new meaning in your life.

Consider this: when you judge a circumstance as "bad," you rob it of its potential to ever be good. Remember that nerdy kid in third grade? He was always nerdy because everyone gave him that label. He never had a chance to not be a nerd. By slapping a negative label on a circumstance, you force a negative meaning on it and keep it from ever having a shot at being a blessing in disguise. How many beautiful lessons have you missed because of a judgment you place on it? Every circumstance, everything that happens to you has the potential to be good or bad. You are the label master.

We all know a blessing can be a curse. If you don't believe me, look no further than people who win the lottery. Many of them go broke within a matter of a few years. And can't a curse also become a blessing? How many businesses and world-changing ideas have been born in the ugly depths of a recession or crisis? Rock bottom can be a solid foundation for success to take place. Or it can be the springboard from which a new leader emerges.

So what's the difference? What determines which label you will attach to your circumstance? Since we're all going to experience challenges on a regular basis throughout our lives, what makes it so some people aren't even phased by their challenges while others are devastated by them? The common denominator is your mind.

When your mindset is bulletproof, you've strengthened it to the point where no outside force can penetrate your thinking. In other words, your mind is "protected" against the worst life can throw at you. Imagine the confidence you gain knowing nothing can take you down from the inside.

Nelson Mandela spent 27 years of his life in prison, most of it alone. During that time, he missed raising his children. He missed birthday parties, game nights, and family reunions. His mother and his son passed away and he wasn't allowed to attend either of their funerals. He was finally released at age 72, about the time most people are beginning to throw in the white towel. After all, what could you possibly do when you're that old and you've missed so much? Yet four years later, he was elected president of South Africa.

How could someone go from nearly three decades of imprisonment and isolation to the highest office in the country in that period of time? Mandela's secret was how he kept himself going all those years. He had little access to even some of the basic necessities of life, but he relied entirely on the one asset he did have: his mind.

How would you see 27 years of being unjustly imprisoned against your will, subjected to horrific circumstances? Tough to cast a positive light on something like that But for Mandela, it was a blessing, not a curse. After his release, he reflected on his time in prison as a "tremendous education in patience and perseverance." It was an opportunity for him to get to know himself and to learn how to use the power of his mind to rise above his circumstances. Later, he reported, "As I walked out the door toward the gate that would lead to my freedom, I knew if I didn't leave my bitterness and hatred behind, I'd still be in prison."

Why go from one prison to another? Why would that make any sense? What good would a life of bitterness have done for him? Mandela knew holding on to negative thoughts and feelings would only make him worse. He who holds the mud gets the dirtiest. Instead, he had developed a bulletproof mind that could not be penetrated by even the worst of circumstances.

Countless other stories throughout history reveal how some flourish from their trials while others self-destruct. What is the common denominator? The strong survive because they have the mental fortitude to thrive. They know how to direct their thoughts toward a positive outcome and release the ones that don't serve them. Learn to embrace your trials and be grateful for them, for they are some of your best lessons in life.

PRACTICE MAKES HABIT

When you do something long enough, you're bound to get good at it. This law also applies to stinking thinking. Think of it. You were born in a specific place in the world, during a certain time in history. You were born with certain genetic tendencies and physical attributes embedded in your DNA passed along from your parents. Maybe you're a "product" of the '50s, '60s, '70s (where the best music came from), or '80s. Or newer. You were raised a certain way, in a certain culture, with two, one, or zero parents. You might come from the streets of downtown Los Angeles, or from a small, podunk town in Iowa, raised on a farm. You may have been born with a lifelong illness or physical limitation. Perhaps you are the oldest of your siblings, the youngest, the only child, or the dreaded middle child. Maybe that's become the label you've lived into, attached to you by others at first and, eventually, yourself.

The list of variables could fill the pages of this book and a hundred more. Each day carries with it an element of risk, which is nothing more than an opportunity to grow (if you choose to see it that way). After all, challenges are simply tests to see if you're ready to advance to the next level. Obviously, there's no secret formula applicable to every single person. If there were, it would be a lot easier to achieve your wildest dreams.

Instead, you get a list of principles to apply, along with the potential for failure in the very pursuit of the prize. When followed, true principles will improve and enhance your life. They are as predictable as the law of gravity. You have to practice the result you want.

SUCCESS IS AN INSIDER'S GAME

If an atom is made up of 99.9999% energy and only .00001% mass, maybe we are all focused on the wrong things. Maybe a door isn't just a door, but a collection of certain types of atoms that are clustered together in the shape and texture of something we collectively have decided is a door. Maybe you can see the chair you're sitting in as a massive collection of subatomic particles, composed mostly of energy.

Aren't you made of atoms as well? What if you saw yourself as mostly energy, being affected by other bodies of energy you come in contact with every day. Remember, when we change how we see things, the things we see will change. Not the other way around.

Many of life's variables are affected by your external environment. But what starts out externally eventually works its way inside you, becoming part of who you are. Regardless of the list of circumstances (good and bad) you were handed at birth, there is one thing you'll have to master if you're going to achieve any level of success: your mind. Success is first created inside you and your external world follows. And it all starts with how you see your circumstances.

Think of the meaning of the phrase, "all in." When you say you're all in, you mean you're 100% committed to something. There's not a shred of doubt. Nobody ever says they're "all out." It's because the most important stuff happens inside you. Stuff like commitment, tenacity, habits, routines, faith, hard work, determination, and a positive mindset. It's the stuff nobody can see but you. That's why only you can truly know what you're capable of. What's happening inside you is much more important than what's happening outside of you.

Now that you understand your mind is being programmed, take some time and clean up your environment. For example, rather than scrolling past people who post things that do not fit your new thought standards, pause to unlike, unfriend, and otherwise unteach social media platforms what is acceptable to you. It's up to you to control your social media, not to be controlled by it. You're either going to use it as a tool or you will become the tool—it's up to you. In time, your feed will transform from a negative river of muck to crystal clear waters that nourish your soul and beautify your mind. There is plenty of goodness out there to fill your "feed" with mental vitamins.

Who are the friends you spend the most time with? What do you do with your downtime? What types of books and movies do you watch most? What do you listen to on your radio? What newsletters do you subscribe to? What does your social media feed look like?

If you're not proud of your answers to these questions or if they are not supporting the type of person you'd like to become, they will always keep you from getting there. It's up to you to make the change; in fact, you're the only one who can.

Feel free to tear this sheet out
and color it as you listen to the
audio, available at:
www.MakeLifeMatter.com

Inspire others by posting finished
coloring pages with hashtag:
#MakeLifeMatter.

CHAPTER 3
Why Your Brain Matters

Ask 100 people, "*who are you?*" and you'll get 100 different answers. Some might give it little thought and respond with their names. Others may list out qualities, talents, skills, or other characteristics they have acquired. On social media, you'll see people who define themselves by their lavish lifestyle, fashion, or number of followers.

Let's answer the question from a biological perspective: you're a series of complex systems composed of hundreds of billions of neurons, a hundred thousand miles of blood vessels, and 30 trillion cells, each containing a hundred trillion atoms. Give or take a few. Maybe you think of yourself as DNA, which, if you unwound it, would wrap around the solar system twice (I'm not sure who actually tested this out, but I want to see photos). If you were a biological recipe, 99% of your ingredients would be oxygen, carbon, hydrogen, nitrogen, calcium, and phosphorus. Under a high-powered microscope, you would see that you're 99% energy, 1% physical matter.

Perhaps you define who you are by your personality. Maybe you have your mother's kindness and your father's humor (dad jokes are the best). You might have more friends than anyone at your school or maybe you just have one: a good book.

A religious person would consider himself a child of a loving

God, with unlimited potential, endowed with seeds of greatness. You're a spirit having physical experiences, as opposed to a human being having spiritual experiences. A walking, talking miracle.

With so many answers to that question, it can be difficult to know where to start. So, let's start with who you are NOT:

- You are not your body, however, you have a body.

- You are not your talents, however, you have more talents than you think.

- You are not your labels, however, others will always slap them on you.

- You are not what you eat, however, what you eat becomes you.

- You are not your habits, however, your habits dictate your results.

- You are not your mistakes, however, you make them every day.

- You are not your failures, however, you experience failure throughout your life.

- You are not your past, however, your past has gotten you to where you are today.

The question remains, then, *who are you?* It's not the easiest thing to answer. Your answer contains your purpose. When you truly come to know for yourself who you are, you live life in a whole different way because you *bring* meaning to every moment instead of trying to find it. If you haven't spent time pondering this question and listening to the answers that will come during quiet moments of meditation, now would be a good time.

As for me, I am a child of God, endowed with seeds of greatness. A unique intelligence, clothed with remarkable biology and the power to perform miracles in my life and those around me. I am an energy, intrinsically connected to other life around me with the purpose to love, serve, give and create each day.

Consider the world around you and how you are interconnected to everything, including nature, animals, the weather and the ecosystem. Everything serves a purpose and works in harmony for your good. Your life is constantly being affected by your environment.

Here's an interesting experiment (although you may find yourself down a rabbit hole, so beware). Try google searching for a phrase: would we survive without _____. Type in different random words and skim through some of the results. Now put in things you think are least likely to be valuable to you and take a look at what you see. It may shock you that things you thought were insignificant are truly remarkable. You may even find yourself feeling a deeper sense of gratitude for things like dirt, bacteria, flies, the moon, spiders, and rainforests. You'll walk away with an enhanced awareness of how interconnected you are to everything else. Who would have thought you could appreciate something so yucky as a worm? What made the difference? Awareness.

Awareness is simply a conscious discovery of what's already there. The world has provided everything you see around you today. All the technology, devices, gadgets, gizmos...it's always existed as a possibility, back in the days of cavemen. For millions of years, it was waiting to be discovered. Man didn't "create" any of it. All we did was organize existing matter into new forms. The more we became aware of scientific truths, the more we were able to "discover" and bring life to new ideas, inventions, and methods that have shaped our world over the centuries. The only difference was hundreds of years ago, it only existed as potential. It was simply waiting for someone curious enough to discover the formula.

Let's look at an example. 100 years ago, cell phone technology didn't exist. Yet, the possibility of it has always existed. It's only because we discovered the right formulation of existing scientific laws and raw materials that we brought the technology to life. Therefore, what may seem impossible today could very well become a common household item for our grandchildren. Everything, it seems, exists as potential at all times. It is our privilege to discover and unveil it.

There's no more transformational state of mind than when you become aware of the opportunities around you and your true potential to use your mind for good. Which begs the question: what other miracles, then, are lurking below the surface, just waiting to be discovered? What miracles will you perform once you discover who you truly are and unapologetically live accordingly?

YOU'RE UNDER THERE SOMEWHERE

A few years ago, my wife suggested we purchase a couple of used dirt bikes for my son's graduation present. The only problem was, one of the bikes needed a little TLC and neither of us had any idea what to do with them. But we looked cool pretending. Thank goodness for YouTube!

I wanted my son to be happy with his gift, so I spent a Saturday afternoon cleaning it up and detailing it as best I could. It was a beautiful, bright blue color, but the rear fender had faded considerably from sun exposure. I ran to the store, picked up a few grades of sandpaper, and went to work on it. Several hours and a few blisters later, the fender was back to its original color and matched the rest of the bike. Nice, little wax job to finish it off and it was as good as new.

Interestingly, the fender was not faded because the paint had worn off. There was no paint; the fender was already a blue plastic. I'm no chemical fenderologist. All I know is that YouTube said I should buff it down. So I did. Like magic, the gunk came off and blue came out.

But something struck me and a powerful lesson emerged: *the blue had been there the whole time*. It was never NOT blue. Blue was the fender's true self. If I had painted it red, it would not have changed its blue nature. *All I needed to do was remove the gunk that was getting in the way of the blue and let its true color show through.*

Imagine trying to define yourself by a label you or others place on you, without your permission. Label by label, one seemingly insignificant thought at a time you begin to limit your beliefs as your true self slowly gets covered up. Remember the 50,000 thoughts you have every day? How many of them are positive? Many of them are flat-out lies. Some of them are downright offensive; things your enemy wouldn't even say to you, let alone your friend. Yet you do it to yourself every day. And you let yourself get away with it. Now you know why so few people have a solid self-image.

What limiting beliefs do you have about yourself? Think of the top two or three and then ask yourself this question: are you REALLY as bad as you say you are? Would others say that same thing about you in that same degree of intensity? Your mind is the great exaggerator. It inflates everything to a greater degree than it actually is in real life. The ultimate drama queen.

Slowly but surely, you develop a crusty shell that keeps you from believing in your dreams the way you did as a child. Somewhere along the way, life beats you down and you start second-guessing yourself. You talk yourself out of living boldly and the thought pattern eventually becomes a habit, a way of life. And when you're surrounded by others whose paint is also covered in gunk, it becomes easy to justify anything inside your mind. It's just the evidence your brain needs to avoid feeling guilty.

Sadly, most of the world lives their lives this way. But we're not here to talk about the rest of the world. This is about you. Maybe you're faded from a tough set of circumstances. Maybe your true colors haven't been able to shine through in years. And maybe you just need a good buffering session from someone willing to risk a blister and some sore joints on a Saturday afternoon.

You are uniquely qualified to inspire others with your own life story. Consider this: right now there are between seven and eight billion people in the world. Not a single one of them has a story identical to yours. That makes you at least one in seven billion; better odds than the lottery offers! You might not think your story matters much, but that's only because you've lived it so long you're used to it. The sizzle has worn off. But what's mundane to you is exciting to someone else discovering you for the first time. You don't have to inspire the whole world. But as you boldly step out from the comfort of your shell and into your element, others will be inspired to follow and you will begin to change the lives of those around you. By courageously living your authentic self you automatically inspire others around you to do the same. People everywhere are starving for such a nudge.

Think about the marvel of technology. You can pick up a palm-sized device that "wakes" up automatically, tap a few places on the screen, and instantly be connected with someone on the other side of the world. Your image is portrayed through time and space in real-time to that one person because he is the only one on the planet who is dialed into your same frequency. This capability has always been available to us, we just hadn't discovered it. When we invented mind-blowing technology, we were not writing new laws of science and math, we're discovering them and learning how to use them to our benefit. Those laws are truths that have always existed and always will. And no amount of denying them will change that they exist.

Likewise, your worth has always existed and always will. You cannot change how valuable you are. Because you are a human life, your worth is invaluable. It's a law, a truth. No amount of bad decisions will ever alter the fact that you are God's greatest miracle. Whether you have discovered this fact or not is irrelevant. However, once you discover it, your life will never be the same.

If you and I could sit down together for just a few minutes and I could impress upon you just one single concept, it would be this: you are under there somewhere. A walking, talking miracle. Your worth was already determined before you were even born. It cannot be changed, not even by you. Not even if you wanted to change it. Nothing you could ever do or say–nor anyone else for that matter–can ever change your worth in any way, shape, or form. No amount of not living up to your potential can make you worth less than you are.

If you don't believe this truth, I urge you to write it down, tape it to your mirror, tattoo it on your forehead, and force your brain to adopt this belief. Brainwash yourself. Make it part of your core to believe that no matter what, you matter. Your life matters. And it always will. Period, end of sentence. Level one is you believing this truth about yourself. Level two is when you believe this truth about everyone else. We'll talk more about that later.

Now, that's not to say you won't make some mistakes along the way. Of course, you will. But truly knowing how much your life matters will change how you go through life. Sand down your gunky layers hard enough and your true colors will shine through like a buffed fender. You were under there the whole time– you just needed to get out from under all those thoughts (and labels). When you do, the world will begin to notice.

THE WORLD'S FASTEST SUPERCOMPUTER

For decades now, scientists, engineers, and IT gurus all across the world have been racing to create a supercomputer that will rival the brain. And since the 60s, we have broken the record and set a new benchmark a couple of dozen times.

When it comes to speed, it looks like we're gaining serious headway. But first, a quick lesson and some new vocabulary. When it comes to measuring computer speeds of significant magnitude, experts have tossed out calendars and even stopwatches. Only FLOPS will do, or FLoating point Operations Per Second. It's just some fancy system to make the rest of us have to learn one more thing.

Now, stay with me as we climb the ladder. A kiloFLOP (kFLOP) is a thousand FLOPS, or floating-point operations per second. A megaFLOP is a thousand kiloFLOPS. After that, we have a giga, tera, peta, exa, zeta and yottaFLOPS, all increasing by a factor of one thousand times greater than the level previous. So a kiloFLOP is ten to the third power, and a yottaFLOP is ten to the 24th power. Make sense?

As of his writing, sources report the fastest computer on record computes at a speed of up to 200 petaFLOPS, or 200 X ten to the 15th power. I have no idea what I just said (I was an art student, not a math student). And I'm sure some really smart guy is going to correct me on social media. But just know that we can all agree...it's pretty fast.

In contrast, it's been estimated that the speed at which a human brain operates is anywhere from a teraFLOP (10 to the 12th power) on up to two levels beyond a yottaFLOP (or 10 to the 28th power). It's a speed for which we apparently don't yet have a name. Any suggestions? I'm thinking bellyFLOP.

So is the computer as fast as the brain? Likely, we're not even close yet (by a factor of many thousands). But for the sake of argument, let's give mankind an enormous benefit of the doubt, and let's say we created the ultimate machine that matches the speed of the human brain. Hold that thought (among your 49,999 other thoughts) as we consider a few additional factors.

For this comparison, I will use research from one of the recent fastest supercomputers in the world: SUMMIT, born in November 2018, complements of IBM.

- Size: The Summit takes up over 5,600 square feet (the size of two tennis courts) and weighs in at 340 tons

- Energy Required: This marvel draws 13 megawatts of energy, resulting in so much heat that it takes 4,000 gallons a minute to keep the machine cool, which is actually considered to be very efficient for a machine of this magnitude

- Contents: 185 miles of fiber optic cables and 4,608 servers

- Cost: $200 million smackers (heck of an upgrade from your laptop)

Those are mind-boggling numbers. Difficult to even comprehend, but I'd like you to try as we now look at the same data points for your brain:

- Size: 15 centimeters long, 3 pounds. Not much larger than your two fists together.

- Energy Required: 20 watts or half the energy of the

average appliance light bulb

- Contents: 100 billion neurons, 100 trillion connections

- Cost: free!

So, even if research is skewed and we're half right, computer technology doesn't hold a candle to the human brain. And here's the best part: you have one of these amazing superduper computers of your very own. Given to you by God Himself. You have 100% private access to it 24/7–*unless, of course, you choose to give away some of that access to others.*

And not to mention efficiency. Thanks to your reticular activating system, your brain is a powerful filter. It shifts the vast majority of your thoughts down to a lower chamber, leaving only that which is of most importance for your conscious mind. In fact, your brain's processing speed is only 50 bits per second, much slower than a computer simply because your brain is able to eliminate everything that doesn't matter, leaving only that which does. That's why you can see very little detail of what you don't look directly at. Try to read even big, bold letters on a sign while focusing on a space next to it.

Think of it like this: everyone loves the idea of winning the lottery. Unfortunately, we think it has to do with money. But what if we redefined it and allowed our minds to dwell on this new idea that if you have a working, functioning brain of your very own, you've essentially won the lottery because there are few limits on what you can do with that thing. Remember, you're one in more than seven billion! And you started out one in 300 million (the average number of sperm who didn't make it).

You, dear reader, have won the lottery. But maybe you just don't realize it yet. What if you're holding the winning lottery ticket but didn't catch the announcement on TV, so you never cashed it in? A winning ticket is a winning ticket, whether you know it or not. It's just waiting for you to claim the prize. I'm giving you permission to claim it. However, you can't just sign the form and watch the money land in your account. This lottery comes with some work to make it valuable.

WHAT BRAINS HAVE DONE

History is rich with examples of remarkable achievements developed and orchestrated through the power of the human brain. Brains have invented, developed, and moved humanity forward in remarkable ways. One brilliant brain after another takes what previous brains have left behind and builds civilization up to new heights of achievement.

It was someone's brain that first thought of the idea to build a pyramid in ancient Egypt. Other brains discovered gravity and formulated complex math equations that have changed how we understand the world around us. Athletes use their brains to envision and achieve world records. They have been known to negotiate with their bodies to do things never thought possible, like breaking the 4-minute mile. Inventors use them to create products formerly considered impossible. Musicians use their brains to create music that speaks to our souls. The list goes on and on. Anything and everything you see around you first germinated somewhere inside the complex neural pathway system of someone's brain.

No matter how old you are, your brain is a supercomputer. You can use it to think thoughts every single day. You can use your computer to consciously choose any thought you wish and hold it in your mind for as long as you like (although it may take some practice). No other species has this type of control. In fact, the degree to which you can consciously choose thought is what sets you apart from all other animals.

Every species has some kind of a superpower. Some can swim across oceans, some can fly. Others have the ability to light up their butts (that's one of my favorites). You cannot do any of those things. But your superpower places you at the top of the food chain. You have the ability to direct your thoughts to alter your state of consciousness and ultimately influence how you act and feel. That three-pound lump of fatty tissue mounted on your shoulders is the most complicated and marvelous thing in the universe. What are you doing with your thinker?

YOUR LIFE MATTERS

Where does a fish learn how to swim? It sounds like a ridiculous question. But there's a wonderful lesson behind asking.

Nobody teaches a fish how to swim. They're born with that knowledge. Everything about them is designed in such a way that they are able to glide effortlessly through the water: their slick bodies, the position of their eyes, their gills and how they breathe, their fins and tails...everything.

The same idea applies to every animal in existence. They all receive their instructions inherently. A calf will learn to walk, a frog will learn to hop and a bird will learn to fly. It's built into their DNA and they just know. There's no such thing as a bird that tries to fly, can't figure it out, and gives up. Or a lion who just can't figure out how to hunt and chooses to be a vegetarian.

You were born with the inherent knowledge of what it takes to do what you are destined to do. So why do so many fail and accept a quiet life of mediocrity? Why, with such a remarkable tool, do so many of us fall short of our dreams? Ironically, it's the same answer: your conscious mind. You think yourself out of your own destiny. You allow negative thoughts, fears, behaviors, and habits to inhibit you from reaching your potential. You take the same powers from this incredible gift and use them on yourself to your own disadvantage! Your superpower can also be your greatest enemy.

Why would you allow such an awful thing to happen? Simple: your brain came with no instruction manual. And unless you learn how to harness its power, that winning lottery ticket you bought sits in your drawer. Have you ever talked yourself out of an opportunity because it makes you uncomfortable? Your mind is the one thing that makes or breaks you. When a fish learns to swim, there's no conscious thought with which it can choose to decide not to. But you and I are given a much greater gift than a fish. The gift of agency to choose success or failure.

You were created by God. You are His child and He is your Father. You have heavenly genes inherently within you. You were born with seeds of greatness. It's in your makeup, your DNA. Your body is a walking, talking miracle and your mind is far greater than the fastest supercomputer in the world will ever produce. Why would you ever question your worth?

Never again underestimate what you have a hold of. Your brain is the control center for your body and habits. And your mind is a broadcast station that sends out signals and attracts the very things you believe and desire most. There's a new sheriff in town, my friends. The mental pandemic is about to come to an end.

*Feel free to tear this sheet out
and color it as you listen to the
audio, available at:*
www.MakeLifeMatter.com

*Inspire others by posting finished
coloring pages with hashtag:*
#MakeLifeMatter.

CHAPTER 4
Brain vs. Mind

Let's understand the difference between your mind (intelligence) and your brain (biology). We'll start with that incredibly efficient three-pound slab of tofu. It has a specific weight and size. It's a tangible object you can physically hold in your hands (although you may not want to). Your brain is a vital organ, is susceptible to disease, injury, and other imperfections of mortality. It's the physical address where your mind resides.

Your mind is non-tangible. It's part of the eternal nature of self. You can't hold it in your hands and it cannot erode or decay. Your mind is perfect intelligence, clouded only by the limitations allowed by yourself and others around you. When you talk about your mind, you use verbs such as think, feel, remember and dream.

UNPACKING YOUR BRAIN

If you could crack apart your skull, you would hold a three-pound lumpy mass of grey matter about 15 centimeters long, about the size of a dolphin's brain. Or, put both of your fists together to get an approximate idea of its size. This wondrous piece of technology (AKA your brain) comes preloaded with software (mind) that runs everything automatically, by default. Your brain is made up of three main parts: the cerebrum, the cerebellum, and the brain stem.

Your cerebrum is the largest part of your brain. It's made up of two hemispheres, appropriately named right and left, and divided into four lobes. The cerebrum is the part of your brain where you perform higher functions, such as interpreting touch, vision, sound, and speech. It is also responsible for your reasoning, emotions, and learning. Your cerebrum is high class and sophisticated.

Your cerebellum is located underneath your cerebrum. It handles your minor motor activity and muscle movements such as the fine movements of your fingers when typing or playing a video game (gamers love their cerebellums). It is responsible for anything that requires concentration, precision, and repetition. It also helps you maintain good posture and balance.

Finally, your brain stem acts as a relay center between your brain's other two main parts and your spinal cord. It is responsible for many of your automatic functions such as breathing, regulating your heart and body temperature, controlling your wake and sleep cycles, digestion, sneezing, coughing, vomiting, blinking, swallowing, and a host of other things you do without thinking about it.

Of course, your brain has many other parts, features, and functions. The purpose of this book is not to provide a comprehensive anatomy lesson. But it is important to lay the groundwork from which we can draw a deeper understanding and appreciation for how it affects your mind.

YOUR PRIMITIVE BRAIN

When you were created, your brain was developed to provide a few basic functions. Some refer to this as your primitive brain. It's designed to keep you safe. It craves comfort and avoids fear like the plague. Your primitive mind wants you to stay away from the unknown or anything that does not have a clear outcome. "Why step out?" it argues. "It's dangerous out there where the saber-toothed tigers roam." Instead, your primitive brain wants you to stay in the cave where life is safe and sound (and boring).

Have you ever felt your primitive brain take over? Maybe you've started up a new business venture and the voices in your head start speaking up, "What are you doing? You've never done anything like this before. Why would you risk what you have going for you right now? Can't you just be content with where you are?"

If there's one great lesson I've learned in life it's this: nothing great happens inside the walls of your comfort zone. Greatness is outside of those walls. You have to go against your brain's better judgment. And that's tough. But nobody can blame your brain. It's doing what it was programmed to do. Back in the day, fear kept you alive. It was a good thing. Because of fear, you avoided being stomped to death by herds of wooly mammoths.

Today, fear is a completely different concept. Dinosaurs are extinct. Your world has evolved much faster than your biology. Rarely do you ever face an enemy that may literally kill you. Most of your fear now is false evidence appearing real, a facade. Yet, fear keeps more people from achieving their fullest potential in life than anything else. Fear of failure, fear of success, fear of all your weaknesses being exposed. Your brain feeds on it and uses it to talk you out of all kinds of opportunities in life. And most of those conversations are happening way down deep where you don't even notice that you're being influenced.

Yet fear, when confronted, is a coward. It's the monster you create in your mind and then run from. Like an internet troll, it's a loud bully when seated safely behind a keyboard, but when you face it, it fades like smoke in the wind. Even a cloud can seem like a solid object from a distance. But how much difference does a cloud look when you're flying through it in an airplane?

Fear is an unavoidable part of life. If you're moving toward any worthwhile goal, you will feel one of two main fears: the fear of the unknown or the fear of missing out on what you could have achieved. Don't fall under the guise that you can avoid fear or that you're inferior for feeling it. Instead, embrace fear as a normal part of your journey. Live in such a way that you can look back and say you stepped out of your comfort zone and tried new things, in spite of fear.

The next time you feel fear holding you back, don't blame your brain. It's just doing what it was supposed to do, like a soldier, carrying out orders. It just doesn't know yet that you are in control now. Old sheriff out, new sheriff in.

Remember? You just need to start training it to listen to a new master.

ARE YOU FIXING TO GROW?

Imagine you're in a room. It's a fairly good-sized room with lots of people but not overly crowded. You're the host of a party and your guests are still arriving. One by one they knock at the door and let themselves in. You increasingly grow concerned about the amount of space you have to host all the guests. Apparently, your spouse sent out a few more invitations than you had planned. What are you going to do with all these people? Will you have enough food? You're starting to run out of standing room, let alone have enough seats to accommodate those who want to sit.

The stream of guests keeps flowing in. They're excited and happy to be at your party. Your stress level goes through the roof. You alert the staff to start preparing extra food, double time. Then it happens. You finally reach your emotional limit and muster up the courage to turn away the first guest. "I'm sorry, we just don't have room for you." Then the second and third. Over time, you grow more numb to it but deep down you still don't feel right about it. The looks on their faces don't exactly help. They spent time dressing up and clearing out their schedule just so they could come to spend time at your party. The idea of a get-together sounded so nice. But poor planning and an overly ambitious guest list have turned the dream into a nightmare.

What I have described is called a fixed mindset. When you have a fixed mindset, you live with limits. You place limits on your thoughts, your ideas, your time, even the amount of success you feel you can achieve. When you have a limited mindset, you perceive your success as one slice of a pie: the bigger piece you take, the less there is for others. As a result, you may resent successful people because, the more they take, the less there is left for you. How could someone hoard all that wealth when others are struggling day-to-day? Blue lens, green lens.

I'm not suggesting that sharing is bad. Quite the opposite. But a limited mindset keeps you from opportunities you would have experienced if you had a growth mindset.

Now imagine that same party. The door doesn't let people into your home because there is no door at all. Your dinner party is outside and guests are arriving from all directions. There are no walls, no fences, no borders. They have open opportunities to walk around, mingle and enjoy themselves. Your stress levels remain in check and you even high-five your wife for how many people she invited. "Make sure you bring your kids or a friend." There's plenty of room for everyone.

LET'S GROW!

Nobody describes these concepts better than Carol Dweck. In her book, Mindset, Dr. Dweck diagrams the following list to help you understand where your own

Fixed:	Growth:
I'm a failure	I can learn to do better
You can't teach an old dog new tricks	I can always learn something new
I can't do that	I can't do that...yet
Genius is born	Genius is built
I'm too old for this	How can someone my age do this?
This is just who I am	I can become whoever I want
I can figure this out on my own	I enjoy learning from others
I'm afraid to do that	I'll do that in spite of my fear

mindset is, and ways to shift into a way of thinking that will serve you.

SPEAKING OF THINKING

Now let's unpack a few things about your thinking. First of all, your brain processes upwards of 50,000 - 70,000 thoughts a day. That's a busy pit crew! From the moment you wake up until the last few foggy moments before you drift off to sleep, the relentless barrage of thoughts is as astounding as it is overwhelming.

It begs the question: why? Are we afraid of being alone with our thoughts? If so, why? Do we feel like we must keep a conversation going in our minds? Why do we hesitate to make time for solitude and mindfulness?

Maybe more important questions might be: when did my mind become less important than my body? Why am I not learning to nourish my mind like I do my body? Why do so many of us dislike being alone with ourselves? Likely, it's simply because you're just not used to it. You've been thinking a certain way for so long, anything else feels wrong.

When you wake up, what's the first thing you do? Most of us reach for our phone (which is never more than a few feet away) where you are sucked into the vortex of other people's agendas. Think about it: social media, notifications, emails all contain things OTHER people want you to do for them. They desperately want your attention.

As you get ready for your day, the news plays in the background with "Everything you need to know to start your day" as a recent headline read in my own inbox. You get in your car to begin your commute and turn on the radio. Music, talk, news- all carefully crafted messages going into your brain. Along the way, you pass dozens of billboards, bumper stickers, storefronts, and other signage, every piece designed by marketing professionals to compete for your attention. Everyone wants a piece of the most valuable real estate in the world: the six inches between your ears.

And you're a professional at giving it to them. After all, you're a "consumer," right? You've been one your whole life.

You arrive at the office and your workday begins. "Crazy busy" is the term we love to use these days. Have you ever met someone who admitted, "I'm just sitting around looking for something to do?"

When does it stop? You cram in some errands on your lunch break and get back to the "grind" after your hour is up. Soon as the day is over, you're back in your car where you are told exactly what you need to worry about. You get home and make dinner as more breaking news pours into your mind and all the young minds within earshot. 99.9% of the news will be outdated and forgotten within 24 hours or less, replaced by tomorrow's breaking news. Yet the idea of missing out makes you uncomfortable. What if you can't contribute to the conversation around the water cooler tomorrow?

It's been "a long day" (another popular line we tell ourselves) so you "reward" yourself by zoning out in front of your favorite social media platform. You catch up on all your missed notifications where your mind is "fed" from your "feed." You read comments from thousands of complete strangers (AKA friends and followers). You've never met them and likely never will, yet somehow, you can't go to bed without knowing their opinion. Talk about overconsumption of mental calories. If your mind was your body, you wouldn't fit through the doorway!

By the way, have you ever arrived at the bottom of your social media feed? No. There IS no bottom. Many news sites are now built the same way. Do you think that's by accident? Your brain does not like open loops. That's why sitcoms and movies are written to leave you hanging. They tease you with the first line of a news story and now you want the rest of it. It's the same psychology that keeps you addicted to your feeds.

Every time you mean to stop, you see the beginning of the next shiny object. "Wait, what's that?" How can you resist? How can you NOT know what's on the other side of that click?

Pretty soon your mind has spent another hour consuming instead of creating. You're exhausted. Not because you've done so much, but because you've done so little of what makes you come alive. You've spent your day consuming the creations of others. And just like overeating makes you feel sluggish and bloated, over-consuming social media makes your mind feel the same way.

Inbox, voicemail, text notifications, zings, pings and badda-bings. Every unopened email, every unchecked notification generates curiosity. And so you continue to consume rather than create. Why? Because it's easier. Consuming takes no effort.

It's why movies are so popular. You grab some overpriced popcorn, sit down and someone else does everything while you just sit there and be entertained. It takes no work. How easy is that? Now, I'm not against enjoying an evening at the movies. I'm against not being aware of what's going on. I'm against you being a tool rather than a mechanic.

When are you supposed to have time to think? You're busy. Your phone lights up and buzzes with notices all day long. And yet you seem to have time for them. The truth is you don't "have" time to do anything. You "make" time to do everything that you want to do. The concept of time management is misleading. It's better understood as self-management or prioritization. Time knows no master- it's ticking on whether you like it or not.

YOU'RE NOT THE CREATIVE TYPE?

When I was growing up, I developed a talent for art. I loved to draw and became pretty good at it. Oddly, I noticed that most people equate art with creativity. Over the years, I somehow earned the badge of someone who is creative. I remember thinking how strange and illogical it was when others commented with, "Oh, I'm just not very creative." Or, "I wish I could draw that well."

But those responses just never sat well with me. They didn't feel true. I always felt that if anyone else spent as much time as I did drawing, they would be able to develop their ability to draw, just as I did. The same concept applies to creativity. You were born a creative genius. God's not a consumer. He's a creator and you are his offspring.

Kids are known to be much more creative than adults. What does that tell you? We UNLEARN our creativity. Throughout our process of growing up, we endure limitations, fears, discomfort, labels, and other lies we allow our minds to believe. And one of the side effects is diminished creativity. Not because our minds become less capable, but because our belief in ourselves has decreased.

And the more you walk around saying you are not creative, the more you live into that belief and manifest it in your life. But who cares, right? So what if you're not creative? The problem with that is your mind is designed to produce ideas. It may be a new invention, business idea, process, or even just a new way of thinking about something. Ideas can be as simple as a beautifully articulated set of words. They come into the world in the form of music, art, or formulas. But make no mistake, your mind is the soil in which ideas germinate. Or (sadly) never even take root.

Everything you see around you was first an idea in someone's mind before it was brought to life. Your furniture, appliances, the cars in your garage, your technology, even the clothes on your back. Everything started out as an idea before it became a reality. And guess where that idea was born? Your brain is a factory, not a warehouse. It's meant to produce, not store. When you keep ideas (and other thoughts) in your mind, you're treating it as a storage unit. Yet ideas cannot sit still for long. Have you ever forgotten an idea just moments after it came? If you don't act on them, they ask someone else to bring them to life. Ideas are too valuable, they're not going to sit around waiting for you.

Receive them with open arms and you'll train your brain to receive more. Develop the habit of collecting your ideas. When you get an idea, do something (I like to use Mattercards). Get it out of your mind and onto paper (or the cloud) where it can be referenced later. Read back through them later and you'll find that some of them are great while others turn out to be worthless. You may not do anything with your idea, but I do know this: if you don't record it, you have guaranteed you cannot do anything with it.

While both brain and mind can work for or against your journey to success. Our focus from here will be on your mind, the asset you get to take with you. Your mind is the most remarkable miracle ever. It's a gift directly from God because with it you can participate in the process of creation. With your mind, you can receive, send, participate in and develop ideas and bring them into reality. *How cool is that?*

Feel free to tear this sheet out
and color it as you listen to the
audio, available at:
www.MakeLifeMatter.com

Inspire others by posting finished
coloring pages with hashtag:
#MakeLifeMatter.

CHAPTER 5
Do You Mind?

As incredible as your brain is, it's nothing without your mind, that powers it. Your brain is the slave. It does the work to make the commands of the mind happen. Your mind is the master. How are the two related? Simply put, your mind is consciousness traveling through your brain. Your brain responds to your mind's orders.

For example, as you recognize an old friend, you might describe it this way: a barrage of photons landed on your retina, activating your optic nerve, which then carried an electrical signal to your lateral geniculate body and then up to your primary visual cortex which released signals over to your striate cortex (where the image's color and orientation are determined) and finally to your prefrontal and inferotemporal cortex where the person was finally recognized and the memory retrieved.

"Jerry, is that you?"

That's just some of the work your brain does in just one single instant. Want to blow your own mind? Multiply that work by millions and millions. Technically, that wouldn't blow your mind because your mind already knows this. It's already doing it. Your subconscious mind is built to handle the volume.

As a test, pause briefly right now to notice your breathing.

Do not change anything except your focus. Shift your mind to become 100% aware of your breaths, just for 30 seconds. Block out everything except your breathing. You breathe all day, every day without thinking about it, yet when you pause to consider all that's going on inside you with every breath you take, it becomes nothing short of remarkable.

While your brain is subject to your mind, your mind is subject to you. You get to control your mind, you do not get to control your brain. You can, however, change your brain by changing your mind. For example, you cannot intentionally interrupt or change your brain's process for recognizing an old friend but you can affect how you think about or respond to that encounter. You get to choose what you make it mean. Your brain produces the facts while your mind brings relevance and meaning to those facts.

LET'S TAKE A TOUR

Imagine your mind as a small, humble home surrounded by a lovely picket fence on the outskirts of a quaint village. Nothing particularly spectacular to look at. You could easily drive by it a hundred times and not take notice. But what a peculiar floor plan! On the ground level, the entire floor plan is made up of one single room filled with natural sunlight.

Working on one side of the room is the world's fastest and most efficient crew you've ever seen, operating a giant printing press. Once a sheet of paper is printed, a second team brings it into a much smaller room, comprised primarily of a light table. Each sheet of paper is placed on the light table for a brief moment, after which most are discarded, making space for new ones. When the workers find similar or repeat messages, they stack them into bundles and pile them off to the side. The crew works non stop all day long. The job is monotonous, yet they never complain. They operate with more precision and harmony than an Indy 500 pit crew.

This room is your conscious mind. It is where your thoughts happen. You put each thought there yourself. Sometimes they seem to run without your permission, but ultimately, you are in control. Your conscious mind communicates in the language of thought. Each printed sheet comes onto the light table, for your examination and inspection. If you give it your attention, the crew waits. If you don't, they replace it with the next sheet. Sometimes the workers move the pages through so quickly that you hardly know what's going on. They couldn't care less about how valuable a thought is, only whether it's getting your attention or not. Whether the sheet contains a million-dollar idea or a worthless piece of gossip is irrelevant to them. They're just doing their job and judging is your job.

It's quite an amazing little operation. Everything is going along smoothly when suddenly one of the workers picks up a large bundle, opens a trap door, and tosses it down into the basement. Wait...there's a basement!? Welcome to your subconscious.

From the street, it looked like a single-story home. But your curiosity leads you down the trap door onto a steep staircase into the darkness below. There are no windows and the air is so thick you can chew it. From the looks of things, the basement hasn't been cleaned in years and the thought of exploring gives you the heebie-geebies. But you muster up the courage to move forward. The constant mechanical hum of gears turning in the vast darkness suggests an even bigger operation than you experienced upstairs.

At the bottom, you enter a doorway to a room filled with hundreds of printing machines humming with engineering precision that would make a Rolex timepiece jealous. As your eyes continue to adjust to the dark, you notice endlessly long hallways in every direction connecting thousands and thousands of rooms that go on for miles. Conveyor belts loaded with bundles from upstairs transport them from room to room. There's not a loose screw in the entire operation and there's not a single person to be found. Only a vast, interconnected symphony of tiny unmanned machines on autopilot. It's as spectacular as it is spooky.

Everything in your subconscious mind operates on habit and automation. Down there, all your thoughts run on autopilot. You cannot see them but you can definitely tell they are there. And if you're brave enough to go down there, you can definitely hear them.

The basement handles all the menial tasks you have to do every day, while the ground level operates much more deliberately. One thought at a time to the tune of 50,000 or more every day. And every so often, the trap door is opened and an object is shared from one floor to the other. Up comes an old memory, down goes a new bundle of thoughts (AKA habit). Up comes a negative thought, down goes a new program, made of thought patterns that have turned into habits.

If your conscious mind tried to manage what the subconscious mind did, it would short circuit in an instant. Instead, your conscious mind deliberately handles thoughts while your subconscious mind (the ultimate pack rat) collects and stores everything, good and bad. It picks up everything around you and stores it. ALL of it. The two worlds work in perfect harmony.

YOUR MIND'S JOB DESCRIPTION

Technically, you have a conscious mind, a subconscious mind, and an unconscious mind. Think of an iceberg. The conscious mind is the small amount sticking up above the water, visible to the world. Below the surface are your subconscious and unconscious mind. To keep things simple, we're going to lump the two together. When I refer to the subconscious mind, think of the two minds (below the surface) vs. your conscious mind (above the surface).

If your conscious and subconscious minds had job descriptions, it might look something like this:

Your subconscious mind is responsible for: your habits, patterns, attitudes, long-term memories, beliefs, desires, physical functions, intuition, creativity, values, addictions, imagination, dreams, mental programs, urges, and fears. It makes up 95% of all your mind's activity.

Your conscious mind is responsible for: your awareness, mindfulness, intentional thoughts, logic, feelings/emotions, intellectual functions, short-term memories, wishes, willpower, present moment, and memorization. It only makes up five percent of what your mind does.

YOUR SUBCONSCIOUS MIND

Your subconscious mind is what supervises this complex cerebral process, all within a few bellyFLOPS. Remember, that's pretty fast. It has to go fast because the brain never sleeps. This part of your mind processes thoughts, intentions, reactions, emotions, shapes, colors, and movements every second of every day of your life. It simultaneously runs every part of your body, pumping your heart, flowing your blood, and expanding your lungs in and out to oxygenate all vital organs of your body. Your subconscious is quite independent. It doesn't bog you down with all these hairy details or even ask your permission. You're not even aware of the majority of the work your subconscious does- or you'd die of overwhelm. But remember, you're the master of this house, so you can become aware of any of it at any time.

Suppose I gave you a math challenge: guess the next number in this sequence: 1 2 3 4 5 6 __. What would you say? Hopefully, it didn't take you long. Your subconscious mind works in patterns and this pattern is X + 1. It's instantly recognizable.

Just as predictable as that math problem is your behavior. Your subconscious mind is wired to recognize patterns in what you do and how you think. It likes to predict the next number in the sequence, all based on what you've done previously. Behavior and thought patterns are predictable and familiar.

Your subconscious mind is also your control center. It regulates your heart, temperature, breathing, blinking...everything. You get an itch on your elbow, you instinctively scratch it with your other hand without a thought. That's your subconscious at play. Its main purpose is to lighten the load your conscious mind bears by converting thoughts into habits where they can be automated. It craves efficiency in every area of life. It's your dominant state of mind (your default program) unless your consciousness is engaged.

While we're talking about it, you might just pause to thank your subconscious mind for the long hours it puts in day after day, like a tireless machine. Best employee in the world if you ask me. And as a courtesy to you, your mind filters everything your brain processes and only features those things that are most important to you. Isn't that incredible?

But keep in mind, your subconscious is a love-hate relationship. On one hand, it's amazing because it handles an overwhelmingly high number of tasks simultaneously. Way out of your conscious mind's league with its one-at-a-time functionality. Imagine if everything was left to your conscious mind. It gets busy with a thought and skips sending the breathing signal a minute or so. Oopies, forgot to breathe. Oh, snap, what about the heartbeat? Yeah, don't want to forget that for longer than, say, one heartbeat. What about seeing and hearing? And regulating body temperature, walking, feeling, and talking? If you had to rely on conscious thought for these activities, you wouldn't last a minute. What a miracle you have such a machine.

But your subconscious superpower can also be detrimental. You see, it is designed to form habits, regardless of whether they're good or bad. So, if you don't intentionally use it to create good habits, guess what happens?

It thrives on the shortest distance between two points. It has to because otherwise, it would never be able to keep up with the thousands of commands it must manage.

YOUR CHILDHOOD PROGRAMMING

Up until you're about seven years of age, your brain is operating in a Theta brainwave which is the state of consciousness just before sleep (delta). This is the wave where your subconscious is the most susceptible to change and input. It's also associated with creativity and open-mindedness. As a child, your mind operates primarily from your subconscious (which is why children aren't very logical). All your systems, beliefs, habits, and ways of thinking are still being formed. From that age on, it's much more difficult to make any changes to the way you think. In fact, most of us keep those same thought patterns for the rest of our lives.

All throughout your childhood, your brain is developing systems and processes that ultimately become your default thought patterns. It's like the operating system on a computer- it runs your systems in the background all day long. And many of these thought patterns that serve you perfectly at a young age will sabotage you as an adult. For example, as a child, you may develop the habit of not speaking up because when you did, you got in trouble with your parents. So, you learn that not expressing how you feel keeps you out of trouble. You may even have seen your siblings speak up and regret it later after being punished. Of course, you didn't want that. Naturally, you learned that keeping quiet was the best way to stay safe. So you did and it worked.

But as an adult, it's a different story. Now you're in the workforce. And there's an important staff meeting. Your supervisor announces a new incentive program that upper management has been putting together to reward the team for achieving a big goal. She asks if anyone has any questions. You do, but you don't want to speak up. Why? What if it appears as though you weren't paying attention? What if you get in trouble? Maybe your coworkers will think you're an idiot. Your childhood thought patterns have come back to haunt you.

And so you keep quiet. As a five-year-old, you discovered the world by asking so many questions you drove your parents crazy. Today, you can't muster up the courage to ask a question in a staff meeting. What happened? Somewhere along the way, you learned that asking questions meant you were either dumb or you weren't listening. You learned that asking questions brought punishments and you're better off keeping quiet. So you do. And so do most of the rest of your coworkers.

Haven't you ever been relieved when someone else asked a question you were too afraid to ask? And how did you see that person? Stupid? On the contrary, those who aren't afraid to speak up are seen as courageous to others. So why do we operate our lives on these false belief systems that do nothing more than hold us back? This is why you have to UN-learn many of the ways of thinking you learned previously. The model for a happy, successful childhood is not the same model for a happy, successful adulthood.

Yes, your subconscious is a powerful beast. It runs rampant and can wreak havoc in your life. It likely already has. But it can be tamed. By becoming aware of and directing your attention to things that matter to you, you put your conscious mind where it belongs: in the driver's seat. Your subconscious has no choice but to surrender.

Today, however, *you* are in control. If you are not where you want to be in life, you can no longer blame your parents, teachers, coaches or anyone else. Embrace the belief that your past is perfect because it brought you to this point. Believe that whatever has happened up to this moment in time is irrelevant. It's the only way to move forward (which is all that matters).

From this moment on, right now, you are 100% responsible for all your habits and beliefs. So, grab a 500-watt halogen work light with you and head downstairs. Expose and purge the habits and belief systems that do not serve you and let's employ your conscious mind to replace them with ones that do.

UNPACKING YOUR CONSCIOUS MIND

As powerful as your subconscious mind is, your conscious mind is the one who wears the pants; it just may not realize it. It's up to your conscience to take charge. A passive sheriff will bring about utter chaos.

When you are in control of your conscious mind, thoughts are brought into the room and examined. You decide to allow that thought to stay for a time or toss it out. But the light table is never empty. The instant a thought is tossed out, a new one has replaced it. Fastest pit crew in the world. You will churn through thoughts all day long, like a machine gun. They come and go fast, but the table is never without a thought. It's impossible to think of absolutely nothing at all. Oh, sure, you may try. And just when you think you succeed, you are thinking about how you proved me wrong and thought of nothing. Which is a thought, which means you're not thinking of nothing. Don't you think? :) Likely, you're just UNAWARE of your thoughts because so many have come and gone for so many years.

Ironically, society glorifies multitasking as if it were a badge of honor. Yet, your conscious mind can only entertain one thought at a time.

Take a minute to try the following exercise:

Grab a paper, pencil, and a timer. With your dominant hand, start the timer and write the phrase, "Multitasking is a bad idea" twice, one above the other. Record your time. Next, also with your dominant hand, write the same phrase twice. Only this time, alternate letters for each of the two sentences, again, one above the other. So, you would write the letter M and again below it, then the letter U twice, and so forth. Record your time.

Which took longer? Which looks better?

Not only can you do the task faster, but you can also do a much better job. This teaches us that when we try to perform multiple tasks simultaneously, we end up doing a mediocre job with each of them like a spork. It's not a great spoon and it's certainly not a great fork. It does what my wife would call a "half-butt" job at either task. And that is how many of us live our entire lives. If you're digging for water, don't dig a thousand one-foot holes, dig a single thousand-foot hole.

YOU MAY SPEND TIME BUT YOU PAY ATTENTION

The concept of time is a very interesting phenomenon. The older you get, the more you value time because your understanding of the nature of time increases. I find it fascinating how we talk about it. We SPEND our time on things, just as we do money. Time is also a currency. When you spend it on something, you are exchanging it for something in return: an experience, a memory, a new idea, a paycheck, an emotion or any other number of benefits. A lot has been said about time being the most valuable asset you own. And those who make the claim are mostly right. Time can be squandered or it can be maximized. It's the only non-renewable resource on the planet; you will never get it back.

Yet, time is ONLY the most valuable commodity in the world when you add focus. Combine time with focus and you get something extraordinary, called "attention," compliments of your conscious mind. Let's dive into this a little deeper.

You can spend time doing something you're not even aware you're doing. You can pass the time for hours in a zone, daze, daydream, or just autopilot. If you've ever been on a road trip, you may drive for miles without realizing you're even driving because you're lost in your thoughts. Kind of scary if you think about it. Your attention is anywhere but on your task. Your subconscious has taken over and is running your life...at 65 miles per hour. Until you mix in focus (which comes from your conscious mind), what you did with your time means little to you. For most of us, our bodies are in the present moment and our minds are either fixated on our futures or locked up in our past.

When the task you are doing involves your attention, you snatch that task right out of the dregs of your subconscious mind into the capable hands of the team that runs your conscious program, where you can choose what matters to you and what doesn't. The more you spend your time with focused attention, the more control and influence you will gain over the beast that lives down in the basement.

YOU CREATE YOUR HABITS AND YOUR HABITS CREATE YOU

When your conscious mind repeats a thought or an action long enough, it becomes a habit. And to preserve efficiency, the subconscious mind wraps up that bundle and escorts it down into the basement where there's plenty of space. This frees up your limited conscious mind for new thoughts and actions. The workers are programmed to do their job.

The question is...what's in the bundle?

Good or bad, you get to create your habits. But once they are in the basement, your habits create you. They run the program of your mind, which ultimately becomes the results you get in your life. It's a beautiful, harmonious process that works for everyone.

The only way it may NOT work in your favor is if you are forming bad habits because your subconscious mind doesn't make any judgments about whether or not a habit will serve you. It's completely unbiased. Good or bad, your mind stores your habits and keeps them alive and automated until they're broken or replaced.

The reason your mind is such an important part of your life's experience is that it controls your inner world, which is essentially all you know. How you think comes from a lifetime accumulation of experiences, ideas, thoughts, habits, and actions of others around you. Even your memory is far more creative than it is factual.

When you become the most dominant voice in your world, you begin to take charge of your mind, rather than being subject to programming by collective society. But keep in mind, you've been programmed to think a certain way for years, so unraveling the tangle of wires will take some constant, sustained effort. Be patient with yourself- you're forming new bundles to replace the old ones.

Feel free to tear this sheet out and color it as you listen to the audio, available at:
www.MakeLifeMatter.com

Inspire others by posting finished coloring pages with hashtag:
#MakeLifeMatter.

CHAPTER 6
From Thoughts to Results

When I was a kid, one of my favorite books was written by Dr. Seuss in 1975, entitled, All Because a Little Bug Went Ka-Choo! It wasn't one of his more popular books, but it was a home run to me. I cannot tell you how many times I have read that book. It's a simple, silly story of a small bug that sneezed one day. Under normal circumstances, it would have been an inconsequential event. After all, how significant is a bug's sneeze? But this bug's sneeze launched a sequence of consequences that increased until, by the end of the book, an entire town was in chaos. And it all happened because a little bug sneezed.

What does this have to do with your mind? Everything. Your thoughts are seemingly insignificant events. Just one negative thought won't hurt. Nobody notices. The world doesn't change. You can still be happy and nice with a single negative thought. But what if that negative thought were to evoke an emotion? That emotion results in an action. Action repeated becomes a habit, which becomes a personality and ultimately a way of life.

How important are thoughts? They're the building blocks of your life. That's how important. Ironically, it's very easy to justify your stinking thinking. We can all rationalize a good pity party. But to Seuss's point, a much greater sequence of consequences is set in motion. Unless we disrupt the cycle, we may not like the outcome.

WHAT THE %@#!! ARE YOU THINKING?

Ever stop to wonder if you just overthink things? What if life was more simple? What if, starting today, you just went with your gut and made every decision instantly and completely? Learn, pivot, and keep moving. No second-guessing. No hum-hawing. No polling for answers among your thousands of "friends" on Facebook. No more responding with, "I don't know, what do you want to do?"

Just you and choice. How much time do you think you waste deciding to make a decision and worrying about whether or not someone will like what you choose to do? How much energy is lost vacillating between two choices rather than picking one with your gut and learning quickly if it was the right decision or not? A mentor of mine taught me that he likes to make decisions quickly because that's the only way he can know if he made the right one or not. And the sooner he knows about his choice, the sooner he can correct it.

The trouble with asking others what they think is they just might tell you. We all know how cheap opinions are. You can find them on every street corner and at all the shop doors in between. Just ask the internet- opinions are free and everyone is anxious to give them away. Truth, on the other hand, is much more difficult to come by.

Unfortunately, it's very easy to mix up the two.

There are two types of truth in the world. I like to call them "true" truth and "you" truth. True truth is true no matter what. It comes from God or science (which ultimately comes from God). It exists regardless of who you are or whether you deny it or not. Gravity, for example, doesn't care how much you agree, if you step off the building, you *are* going to fall. Period. It's indisputable. Even if you create a vacuum or go into outer space, gravity still exists and you cannot change it. True truth is black and white.

You truth, however, is a million shades of grey because now your lens is involved. It's your core belief system and it can and does change throughout your life. You start with a set of beliefs from your childhood and alter them as you grow and adapt to new belief systems that feel true to you. Political views are individual truths. They're true to the person who owns them. The good thing is, you get to choose this type of truth.

The majority of what you believe today is you truth. It's a library of ideas, repeated thoughts, belief systems, and core values that "feel" true to you but are not necessarily indisputably correct (although you cannot imagine why anyone else would NOT agree with you). These truths define you and dictate how you react, speak and show up in the world. As essential as they are to you, so are they to the person to your left and right who sees the world from a different viewpoint— their viewpoint.

At the end of the day, we're all the same at our core: we're all spiritual beings, inhabiting and bringing life to an enormously complex cluster of energy, vibrations, atoms, and cells (called a body). We spend our lives altering that state of vibration through our consciousness, discovering ideas from others around us, filtering out the unwanted truths that will not serve us, and adopting the good ones into our lives.

Intentionally building your own belief system is the most important work you will ever do in your life. Your mind constantly thinks; it never stops. In fact, even when you're sleeping, your brain doesn't take a break. Most of the thinking your brain does is inaccurate, flawed, illogical, and even hurtful. Your thoughts are often flat-out lies. Yet you think them, simply because you haven't yet developed your filtering skills. Many of your thoughts have been accepted as truth are actually bald-faced lies simply because they went unchecked at the door. In fact, when it comes to you truth, don't worry about whether your thoughts are true or not. Focus on whether your thoughts will serve you. Because if they do, they will become true to you.

Let's unpack this idea a little more. Suppose you set what we might call an impossible goal for yourself. You can either choose to think, "I've never done that before," or, "I'll keep failing until I achieve it." Both thoughts are equally true. The first one starts you on a path of doubt, fear, and self-limiting beliefs. The second has a confidence and determination to it that will greatly increase your odds of successfully reaching your goal. The question isn't which thought is true. The question is: *which thought best serves you?* You can apply this formula to any new thought that wants to enter into your domain.

But don't blame yourself if you haven't mastered your thoughts just yet. You certainly weren't taught that skill in school. Instead, you're taught to cram information into your brain, memorize it through repetition and later identify it among a list of other answers designed to trick you. You memorized, regurgitated (and likely forgot) the information you learned. A letter grade at the top of your paper displays how well your short-term memory has performed but is no indication of how well you have truly learned the material.

You're only going to learn how to think by absorbing it from others who have done it well. Thinking comes from intentionally observing your world and the people around you and then forming your beliefs from what you've observed. Until then, you're a sponge, soaking up the thinking from others around you. Put another way, until you learn to think for yourself, others will do your thinking for you. I call it surrogate thinking. And there's no shortage of bad thoughts out there eagerly waiting to seep into your subconscious.

MIND, BODY, SOUL

Your mind is the boss. It's the epicenter of the earthquake. Habits, actions, motivation, intention...everything stems from your thoughts. So where do thoughts come from? Do you have any say in the matter or does your brain automatically insert thoughts in your head? I know of only three sources where your thoughts can come from.

First, your circumstances or environment. What's going on around you can "spark" a thought. Granted, it's still your mind that formulates the thought, but something in your environment can spark your thoughts. Let's say you're walking down the street on your lunch break. It's a beautiful day and you're enjoying the breeze...with a little vehicle exhaust mixed in. Your thoughts are drifting along, fantasizing about an upcoming family vacation you've been planning. All of a sudden the screech of a nearby vehicle interrupts you, followed by a loud, horrific crash. As you look toward the noise, the smell of burnt rubber stings your nostrils. What just happened to your thoughts? Vacation? What vacation?

The second-place your thoughts come from is your beliefs from your past. All through your childhood you develop and build a belief system. Much like your immune system, your belief system is also built through interaction with others. Parents, friends, coaches, teachers...anyone you look up to or hold in a position of authority (which, when you're little, is just about everybody). Things they say, especially when mixed with emotion, can make a profound and lasting impact on your nature, your personality, your fears, and self-limiting beliefs, how you think, how you react, everything. These belief systems are built all throughout your childhood, especially the first 10 or so years of your life. Unless it gets checked, this belief system will direct the results you get throughout the rest of your life.

The third-place your thoughts can originate from is yourself. Your conscious mind has the ultimate power to think any thought you want. You are in control and you can think an exact thought whenever you want for however long you wish to think it. What an amazing freedom you have! Technically, the other two sources of thought come from you as well, just indirectly. But this source is different. I'm talking about intentional, deliberate thought.

Your mind is so powerful that your body even obeys it. We've talked about the subconscious mind controlling all of your movements such as your breathing and heartbeats. But your body can also memorize movements (called muscle memory) that it repeats inadvertently.

OLD RUTS DIE HARD

In our bathroom, my wife and I have two sinks. Next to each is a small medicine cabinet behind a mirror each of us uses for personal hygiene and care. One day, I noticed my wife using my side of the sink. After asking her about it, she explained the setup was easier for her to access because of the location of the outlet and mirrors. I suggested we simply change sides, which we did. For the next 2-3 weeks, I repeatedly stepped out of the shower and opened my old mirror, only to see my wife's makeup.

Of course, I knew we had changed sides, but it took my body some time to catch up to the idea. In essence, I had to create a new habit to replace the old one. We had been used to using one side and as soon as we switched sides, my body continued doing what it had been trained to do. This happens all the time- likely more than you are aware. Have you ever seen someone hold up a phone and pretend dial with their index finger just to remember a phone number? Muscle memory.

Your mind is in charge of your thoughts. Your thoughts become actions (body) and emotions (soul), which is your body's response to the thought in your mind. That's the grand trio that runs your life. Mind, body, and soul, with the mind at the helm.

Both actions and emotions can become habits. Initially, they start out as a reaction, but when repeated over time, they turn into something that runs on autopilot.

How often do you have to clean your room? There are two ways to operate: first, keep your room clean and never have to clean it, or second, live in a continual loop of messing it up and cleaning it. It's a simple matter of your habits. When you take your shirt off at night, where does it go? If your habits support a clean room, it goes in the dirty hamper or back in the drawer or hanging in your closet. But not on the floor. Everything has a place and this habit requires taking the time to put it in its place rather than leave it to be done later, which never happens. One item at a time and your room can go from tidy on Saturday morning to a war zone by bedtime.

In what areas of your life could you use some new or better habits? You might say, I'm not good at forming habits. Actually, you are a natural-born master at it-you've just formed the wrong ones. For example, NOT keeping your room clean is a habit.

Your habits may not be good ones, but make no mistake, you are wired to form habits. Rather than worrying about your ability to create new habits, focus on refining or replacing the ones you have. Trust your ability as the habit expert you already are. It just takes some brainpower and consistent effort.

I recommend starting small. Pick an action that is so small you cannot fail. If making sales calls every day is a habit you need or want to develop, don't start out committing to a thousand. Commit to ten, or even just one. There's time in anyone's schedule to make just a single phone call. One call is easy enough, right? Get that down and grow the habit from there.

Set big goals and invest your energy in the small, daily steps that will eventually get you there. Action is great but consistent action is like compounded interest in your investment account. You have to be willing to take action until the goal is manifest, however long that is.

It's pointless to choose a goal inside your "know" zone. Instead, challenge yourself with a goal big enough that you don't know HOW you're going to get there. If you have no idea how you'll accomplish it, you'll know your goal is big enough. The "how" comes on its own when you get your mindset right and you have no other option than to move forward in faith.

Next, do something that forces your commitment. For example, rather than committing to eating no sugar, which would send some people into shock, commit to serving yourself your normal portion of dessert, cutting it in half, and throwing one half in the trash. You're not likely to reach in and eat it later. But you are likely to finish the dessert on your plate. Change your environment to support your habits and they're much easier to adhere to. You cannot eat a donut that isn't already in the pantry.

Finally, implement the piggybacking method. Rather than forming a new habit from nowhere, create one that goes with another already in your system. For example, maybe you're good at brushing your teeth, but you're not good at flossing. Strap your floss to your toothbrush so you can't help but see it when you go to brush. Commit to flossing just one simple tooth. You're not likely to stop at one, but at least the habit is being developed, it's piggybacking an existing habit and your brain is being molded with new neural pathways to support it, giving you a much greater chance of keeping your habit going.

TALENT IS OVERRATED

There's a process you can follow from thought to tangible results. Once you understand what's going on and what affects what, you are empowered to begin making the necessary changes that will bring about the results you want in life. The first step is thought, but some of your thoughts stem from beliefs acquired through your childhood. So, let's talk about it...

A small percentage of us were born with a healthy dose of raw talent. Nobody knows the exact number but for the sake of argument, let's call it 1% to be generous. I'm always in awe listening to a child sing pitch-perfect before they can even ride a bike. Some have better voices than trained college graduates in music studies (certainly better than me). They can barely read or spell their name, yet they open their mouths and heaven comes out. Yeah, that's just a gift from God Himself. You've seen these kids: gifted in math, reading, science, or the arts. If you didn't get one of those wild cards at birth, there's nothing you can do about it so don't compare yourself to them. Instead, learn to appreciate those gifts and focus on developing your own.

As for the rest of us—the other 99%—we are born as

"regular" people who must fight for and develop our talents the old-fashioned way: hard work and dedication. If you find yourself in this camp, you're very normal. If you're thinking you don't have any special talents or gifts, first of all, you're in the large majority. Second, you just may not have uncovered it yet.

No matter who you are, you have seeds of greatness within you. I don't care if you're seven years old or seventy. You may say that the seeds haven't sprouted yet. And maybe you're right. But that doesn't mean they're not there. It just means you need to get some dirt and water in there and a little sunlight on them. They'll grow. How do I know this? You are a child of God. You were born to manifest His glory and be a light to those around you. He placed you here on this earth with your body, your mind, and unlimited potential. He wouldn't sabotage one of his own children. Of course, He wants you to live the most fulfilled life you can. So He empowered you with special gifts that are yours for the taking. But you likely will have to work to discover and develop them.

Regardless of who you are, you will develop a belief system that will either enhance your God-given gifts or detract from them. That belief system comes in large part from your upbringing. Your parents play a critical role here, but other influencers include friends, teachers, coaches, relatives, neighbors, and more. Things people said, what they taught, your church, your community, your political views- everything is shaped, molded, and formed into who you are up to this point in your life.

But here's the key: where you are today is based on your past, which cannot be changed. But where you go from here is 100% up to you.

Remember the Theta brainwave state? Creativity, open-mindedness, and ideas? There are a few ways we enter this state: meditation, relaxation, or the last moments before and first moments after sleep. This is why our best ideas come to us while driving, in the shower, in early mornings, or on vacation. This also is why successful people do not reach for their phones or check email when they first wake up (experts recommend at least an hour). That first little while as your brain gets going is uber-precious time and should be used to help program your mind for your goals and reprogram your thought patterns. Develop a routine that includes visualization, meditation, exercise, and/ or reading. Use that window of time wisely because as soon as you hit your inbox or arrive at work, it's beta and gamma brainwaves all day long.

Mark Twain once wrote, "It ain't what you don't know that gets you in trouble, it's what you know for sure that just ain't so." What do you "know for sure?" What belief do you hold near and dear that has never been questioned because it's always been with you?

YOUR MIND LOOP

There's a process that goes directly from thought to result. You may not realize it but you're an expert at this process. You live it and practice it every day. Here's the process: Your thoughts can come from your beliefs which can also produce more thoughts. When you have a thought, it creates an emotion. Your feelings produce your actions and when repeated enough, actions become habits. Your habits create the results you get in your life, which produce positive thoughts.

In other words, every result you have in your life right now first began as a thought that was repeated long enough to see the light of day. Sometimes you can go through this loop very quickly. Other times it can take years for results to take place. But make no mistake, what you have in your life right now began with your thoughts.

Most people blame outside circumstances for their lack of progress. There's always something preventing them from moving forward: excuses. When it comes to excuses, any one of them is as good as any other because all of them keep you from your dreams. Once you accept as your truth that you and you alone are responsible for your thoughts, you can own every outcome you've had to this point. Once you own your outcomes, you are empowered to change as you move forward because you become the master. You are no longer the victim.

Think of a tree. There are several key elements to any tree:

seeds, roots, trunk, branches, blossoms, and fruit.

Beliefs and Thoughts are seeds. You "inherit" them throughout your youth. As you enter your teenage years, your seeds are formed. Some are good seeds, and you probably have some bad ones in there, too. Spend your attention on cultivating the seeds that will produce fruit down the road. Stop planting weeds and hoping for watermelon. That's a formula for disappointment.

Belief systems are the roots of the tree. They're underground and hidden. A thought repeated long enough or repeated with emotion will become a way of thinking or a belief system. You cannot see them, yet they nourish everything above ground. Remove the root and everything withers. But be careful of the thoughts you repeat because they will become your limitations. But remember, you get to keep all the limitations you fight for.

Feelings are anchored thoughts. Imagine the trunk of the tree. They come directly off of your thoughts and feed into actions for all to see. A thought is neither good nor bad. It's only a sentence until we make it good or bad. When you judge a thought, it fuses with emotion and becomes a feeling.

For example, death in and of itself is not sad to most of us. People die all over the world every day yet we don't walk around constantly crying because of it. However, the death of a close friend or family member is sad because the thought has a deeper meaning.

The thought that you'll never see them again causes feelings of sadness. That's the difference.

The stronger the anchor, the more powerful and intense the feeling you will feel. That's why you can hear someone's name ten times in the last five minutes and still not remember it, yet you can vividly remember a traumatic experience you had when you were six years old. The former was white noise and faded away like fog, the latter was infused with strong emotion and will never be forgotten. You can learn to use this process to work for you by intentionally mixing in your own emotion to anchor your thoughts.

Actions are the branches. Tons and tons of actions, going different directions. Big ones, small ones, broken and crooked. Your actions, like branches, are never perfect. However, step back and look at the tree as a whole and you see something marvelous. The interesting thing about action is it's the best way to learn. Our education system teaches us to learn by consuming, memorizing, guessing, and regurgitating. But the truth is, you learn best by teaching, which is taking action.

Suppose I had two identical, unmarked plastic buckets in the kitchen pantry, one with sugar and one with flour. I asked you to go get me a cup of sugar, what would you do? It's simple- open one. If it's sugar, you nailed it the first try. If it's flour, you know the other one is sugar. Do you consider opening the first lid a failure? Of course not. You see it as the way in which you discovered where the sugar was so you could complete the task.

When it comes to taking action, worry less about what action to take and focus your energy on taking the best action you can with the information you have. If it's wrong, you'll quickly learn and can course-correct sooner than later. Either way, you're moving forward. God cannot steer a parked car.

You've heard of the law of attraction? Basically, you can choose what to attract into your life by your thoughts. Many successful people swear by this law and have written about it extensively over the years. One book (and movie) came out entitled, "The Secret." Fundamentally, it had a lot of truth. For me, however, it focused too heavily on thought and didn't sufficiently emphasize the one core principle that makes the entire secret work. Let me give you a hint:

The Law of AttrACTION

If you notice, more than half of the word "attraction" is "action." Thoughts are powerful things but they're not everything. Unless you take action, you remain stagnant.

Try this experiment: find a video that teaches a new skill (like doing a handstand or riding a unicycle) and watch it ten times a day for 30 days. The following month, try learning that same skill by taking action: practice it ten times a day for 30 days. Compare the results. Nothing replaces action.

Habits are beautiful, fickle flowers on the ends of some of your branches. They can form and be gone instantly. Other habits we carry around for years. You may say you're not good at developing habits but remember: you are a creature of habit. Don't we say that all the time? And it's true. Our brains are wired to accumulate and produce habits any time we can. Remember, our subconscious basement thrives on efficiency, always trying to turn actions into habits.

Typically, we think of habits as new things we learn to do. But there are also habits of omission. What you are practicing NOT doing can be every bit as important as what you ARE doing. If you don't feel like you're good at forming habits, you're wrong. Human beings are innately gifted in this area. You simply haven't learned how to form habits *intentionally*, resulting in the wrong habits forming themselves that you're now carrying around. The new sheriff needs to put his foot down.

Results are the fruit that grows from the blossoms of the tree. If you've taken good care of your tree, the law of the harvest suggests that your efforts will bear fruit. It's the natural outcome of all the previous effort and care.

So what results do you have in your life? Are you happy with them? Maybe you're picking a piece of fruit from the tree and trying to change it. You expected oranges and you got apples. Frustrating, right? Instead, you need to get to the heart of the problem, which begins way back at the seed. What seed did you plant? The law of the harvest is exactly that: a law. You always get what you sow. It might be a long summer but eventually, harvest season will arrive and you will get exactly what you sowed.

LET'S CREATE SOME LUCK

Since everything starts with a thought, it's important to understand how your brain filters out and delivers to you those external circumstances that support or validate your predominant thoughts. Your thoughts (mind), mixed with emotion (body), develop the conviction it will happen. Anticipation is born. When you start expecting results in your life and back them with supporting thoughts and feelings, you get what some call, "lucky." Not because the opportunities magically appeared; they were always there. But because your brain now notices them, enabling you to take advantage of them. Which gives the illusion to the world that you are a "lucky" person.

Luck is a slippery phenomenon, difficult to wrap our minds around. There are times things just happen coincidentally to someone for no reason at all. Like the guy in Vegas who wins the jackpot on his first day at the slots. We all know people who always seem to always get lucky. It's almost as if they never have to struggle or work for things, everything just seems to show up in their lives in the right place and at the right time.

Maybe you feel like that's never been nor ever will be your thing. You're just not lucky like that. Those thoughts may even make you bitter at the world, thinking your deck has been stacked against you. On the flip side, there are those who just cannot seem to catch a break in life no matter what they do. Either way, the opportunities are there. They may not be showing up on your radar because you're expecting something different.

For example, Google search the phrase, "the world is a bad place" and you will find nearly 900,000 hits (as of the writing of this book). That's plenty of evidence to support the thought. One may argue that the thought must be true if so many people agree with it. Now change it to "the world is a good place" and you'll find over 4.4 million hits.

If you stop after the first search, you could easily come to the conclusion that the world truly must be a bad place. There's plenty of evidence, either way, to validate whichever belief you have. But both sets of results prove that the answer lies inside you. What evidence are you seeking to justify and validate your belief? Your brain operates much the same as Google. It shows you results that prove your thought was right. Both sets of results are always there, but one set comes to life when you look for it while any opposing evidence quietly fades into the darkness.

And presto, you have a narrow-minded, one-sided view of the world. You see this all the time in politics. Who wants to look at any evidence that could reveal they are wrong?

While none of us can explain the role of luck in every case, the majority of cases can be created intentionally with hard work and anticipation. The good news is you are 100% able to develop those traits in your life. In other words, it is within your control to significantly increase your chances of becoming lucky. Not Vegas luck, but opportunity luck. God has a way of noticing and rewarding those who step out in faith and put forth the effort. He will bring into your life those concepts, ideas, thoughts, relationships, and opportunities that you need at the time you need them. But you must first prove you're worthy of such blessings through proper effort and mindset.

This process of using the thought loop to attract and generate a certain result in your life is called manifesting. If I were to ask you how good you are at manifesting results in your life, how would you answer? Maybe you're looking around at your life thinking, "based on what I'm seeing, I'm not good at all!" But remember this key principle: \your brain is already wired to manifest and bring to pass things in your life. It already knows how and is already doing it. You're already good at it even though you may not realize it. The difference is, you may be manifesting bad results instead of good results.

Rather than beat yourself up and think you're no good at this manifesting stuff, praise your mind for already having this superpower and begin the process of adjusting your thoughts, beliefs, emotions, and actions to begin manifesting the results you want in your life instead of the ones you don't.

*Feel free to tear this sheet out
and color it as you listen to the
audio, available at:*
www.MakeLifeMatter.com

*Inspire others by posting finished
coloring pages with hashtag:*
#MakeLifeMatter*.*

CHAPTER 7
Your Identity Continuum

Your mind operates along a continuum: past, present, and future.

Your past is made up of facts and evidence. This is your mind's favorite place to visit because your brain craves evidence and predictability and it hates uncertainty (which requires faith).

Your future is made up of faith and imagination. This is a much more difficult place for your mind to spend time because it requires conscious effort and there's no track record. It's fun to daydream, but when it comes to believing in those fluffy dreams, the lack of evidence sends your mind spiraling back to your past where things are safe and predictable.

Your present is made up of who you are right now. This is often the most difficult place for your mind to be because of the overwhelming distractions and noise pulling you in every direction. Most of us fill our minds with so much that we rarely find ourselves being truly present. You might say we're stuffocating.

Let's take a deeper look at these three elements and how you can best use them.

A NEW WAY TO SEE YOUR PAST

The story is told of the old fisherman who went to a nearby river to spend the afternoon fishing in his favorite spot. He put on his wader boots and walked out into the middle of the river where the soft current flowed gently around his legs, keeping him cool from the warm afternoon sunlight. He faced downstream where the water led to a dam. It was a dam fishing hole. OK, sorry for the dad joke.

He baited his hook and cast in his line, giddy with anticipation. A bite. He set the hook and reeled it in only to reveal an old boot. Disappointed, he tossed the boot over his shoulder and cast his line back in the river, downstream. Minutes later, another bite...or so he thought. Again, the same boot. Again he threw it behind him and resumed his fishing. Over and over the old man caught the boot, only to throw it upstream into the river behind him.

Like the fisherman, if you don't let go of your past, you are destined to repeat it. Or, better stated, every time you relive your past, it becomes your present. When your memories are bigger than your dreams, you have submitted yourself to your past.

What kinds of feelings surface as you think about your past? Any regrets? What has happened to you that makes you feel like you're not as good as someone else? Do you find yourself wishing you could go back and change things? Are you carrying around any burdens you should let go of? More importantly, why would you carry those around? What good are they? You know all those mountains you've been carrying? Turns out you're supposed to climb them, not carry them.

The truth is, you're in good company, although that doesn't make it right. Everyone has a past and most of us hang onto it, reliving it constantly throughout each day. Ironically, what that does is tie yourself to an identity, which trains your brain to hang onto that identity, keeping you from becoming someone new. It's impossible to redefine yourself when you're anchored to a previous version of yourself. As you know, your brain wants to be right. So when you're faced with the unknown of becoming someone new, unless you have a strong enough mindset and action to support it, your brain will default into who you were because it's predictable and safe, even though the results fall short.

In other words, when faced with a challenge, we don't tend to rise to the level of our dreams, we tend to fall to the level of our training.

Toss the old boot to the side (up onto the shore), set your sights ahead, and cast your line without fear of catching your past. In order to do this, you need to start by adjusting your mindset. Let me give you a suggestion. Often we don't like our past because our past is not perfect. It's full of mistakes and oh, how we wish we could go back and do it all over again! That thought will never serve you because as of this writing, time travel has not been invented. Instead, adopt a new thought and repeat it long enough until it becomes a belief.

Here is one example:

My past is perfect because it got me to this point.

Whatever your past was does not matter anymore. The good, the bad, the ugly... whatever you did or did not do, you are here now to this point in your life. So let that be what you focus on, not everything you would change. And that's something to be grateful for because this moment in time is when you can alter the course of your life, forging a new trail for a different and better future.

Looking at it in this light, you can now believe your past is perfect because it fulfilled its mission. With the knowledge, motivation, and understanding you are gaining each day, you are now 100% in control of your life moving forward. Other people no longer will have the same kind of effect they have had on your past. The only reason they did was because you didn't know better. But now you do.

So let's agree—your past was perfect because it brought you exactly to this point in time. It serves you to think of it that way. Let's start looking through a better lens. What you've been through will come through what you see through. If you're not intentional enough, your past will dominate by default. It needs only your lack of effort in order to drown out your present and future.

THE PRECIOUS PRESENT

As if your past wasn't enough of a deterrent, there are other challenges battling for your number one place of influence. Your future isn't here and never will be because as soon as it is, it becomes your present. Your past is behind you, never to return again. Right now is all you have. Yet your "present moment" may not be all that present after all.

One of the great pandemics of our day is shiny object syndrome or SOS. This is fitting because anyone with SOS ought to be crying out for help. Consider how many times a day you are interrupted or distracted. Here are some alarming statistics:

- On average, we check our email up to 80 times a day and our phones every 12 minutes or less

- Most of us switch activities about every 3 minutes

- We get interrupted just 11 minutes into an activity and can take up to 25 minutes to get back on track which can cost 4 hours of lost productivity a day

- 80% of interruptions are not important (let this one sink in)

- Multitasking can reduce your productivity levels by up to 40%

There seems to be an endless supply of data that supports the notion that the odds are stacked against you unless you take control of what you allow your mind to think about. Interruptions, distractions, and reactions are not the only byproducts of a lack of mindfulness. Truly, the most valuable thing you can give another person is your attention.

Dr. Matthew A. Killingsworth, a doctor of psychology from Harvard, conducted a study that revealed that 47% of our day is spent on something OTHER than what's going on in our present moment.

"This study shows that our mental lives are pervaded, to a remarkable degree, by the non-present." Killingsworth goes on to report that, "Mind-wandering is an excellent predictor of people's happiness. In fact, how often our minds leave the present and where they tend to go is a better predictor of our happiness than the activities in which we are engaged." The study concludes that a wandering mind is an unhappy mind.

Any time we are not fully present, we are sacrificing something—potentially our own happiness. Mass media and social media outlets have trained our minds into an inability to focus. Have you ever clicked open a new tab on your computer with a specific purpose in mind and a few minutes later you have 12 more tabs open and you've forgotten what you started doing in the first place? Companies pay fat salaries to educated professionals whose sole job it is to get your attention-even if just for a few seconds. It's called marketing and it's everywhere. Unless you develop the ability to become intentional with your focus and thoughts, you will always trade your success for the shiniest object in the room.

Before you can take charge and change it, you must become aware of what's going on right now at this exact moment. It's called mindfulness: the habit of eliminating anything that does not have to do with what's going on right now in this present moment.

Here's a brief exercise that may cause you to experience the start of an awakening. Pause whatever you're doing and dedicate the next 60 seconds to this exact moment. Slow down your breathing and listen to your breaths.

Next, go through your five senses. Listen deeper than you ever have- what do you hear? What do you see that you haven't noticed before? Can you smell or taste anything? What do you feel? If you're sitting on a chair, how does it feel against your back and legs? What else can you feel? The floor, shoes, this book? If you actually set your timer and press pause on everything else, you'll see how you've slowed down time. 60 seconds can feel like 10 minutes.

Speaking of time, do you know why so many people talk about how the years are just "flying by?" Maybe you're guilty of saying that yourself. "Wow! I can't believe it's already April!" "Where has this week gone?" Society even glorifies people who are always on the go.

Time passes by fast when we are not present. Distraction removes us from the effects of time and we lose track. Have you ever lost "track" of time driving and an hour goes by in 10 minutes? To slow down your clock, simply become more present.

Think about the last time someone came up and began a meaningful conversation. How closely did you pay attention? How often did you find yourself thinking of what you'll get back to as soon as the person stops talking? Did you give 100% of yourself or did you split yourself with 3 other thoughts and only give the 25% that was leftover?

No wonder we can't remember things well. Our minds aren't into what we're learning because we're so used to spinning multiple plates. Jack of all trades, king of nothing. Do you think the other person can tell when you're not 100% present? Always looking for the next thing in your day, or trying to do multiple tasks at once will keep you from truly enjoying the present moment, which is the ONLY moment you ever have. Your body lives in one sphere while your mind lives in another. This misalignment deteriorates your peace, happiness, and fulfillment.

Imagine your past as an enormous magnet. It's pulling you back in its direction with a constant, steady magnetic force that never goes away or weakens. It's already programmed to be your default direction. Now imagine your future. It may or may not have such a magnet. It is up to you to intentionally create one. The magnetic force you create toward your future will need to be *stronger* than the one pulling you to your past. If not, guess which direction you will go?

When you are truly present, you're whole with yourself. Complete. Which means you want or need for nothing. Wanting something you don't have comes from a place of incompleteness. Your feeling incomplete results in wanting something you do not have. That doesn't mean it's wrong to want more. Just make sure you want from a place of abundance. Meaning, your completeness doesn't depend on you attaining that thing. You are whole just the way you are. You don't "need" anything more to make you a better you. You're already a freaking miracle just the way you are! Remember?

WHAT CAN YOU DO ABOUT IT?

If you're feeling like you could use some help in this area, here are a few suggestions:

Avoid checking email, or even picking up your phone during the first hour after you wake up. If you're responsible with your money, you pay yourself first. The same principle applies to time, an even more valuable asset than money. Give that precious first hour to yourself. And if you don't have a full hour of morning routine before you leave for work, consider waking up earlier.

Schedule time on your calendar for you. Likely, your calendar is filled with meeting the demands of other people: bosses, spouses, family, friends, coworkers, etc. If you don't intentionally fill your time with what you want and need, the world will fill it for you with the things they want. You become the slave, not the master.

Tidy up your environment and develop supporting habits to keep it that way. A cluttered environment is one of the most common enemies of focus. Toss out any unnecessary documents. When you're finished with something, go through the extra effort of putting it back where it goes rather than tossing it across the back of a chair or piling it on the table. Manage your computer and phone notifications- if they're not essential, turn them off. When you're doing deep work, work in a single tab on your browser and turn your phone to sleep mode.

MEDITATE OR MEDICATE?

Your brain's pharmacy sends out chemicals that aid in giving your body what it needs to stay healthy and well. Thoughts of fear, stress, worry, or self-doubt will block these chemicals. When this happens long enough, you go to the doctor to find out what's wrong and come home with prescription medication that takes the place of what the brain was supposed to do in the first place. Rather than relying on chemicals to regulate what your body needs to be healthy, invest some time into rebuilding your mind and body's ability to heal itself. Of course, there is much more to this than just your thoughts, but a regular practice of mindfulness and meditation is the perfect place to start.

Mindfulness is the general attitude of being aware of your actions, thoughts, attitudes, and emotions in your present moment. Meditation is the intentional practice of being mindful for a specific period of time. When you meditate, you direct your focused thoughts toward a specific purpose or end result. Both are valuable to help you practice being and staying in the present moment. There is a variety of meditations you can practice, including breath awareness, visualization, guided practice, and transcendental.

Sadly, it is estimated that less than 15% of us practice meditation at least once a year. Yet the following are just some of the benefits researchers have discovered. Meditation can:

- Reduce the wake time of people with insomnia by 50%

- Reduce symptoms of post-traumatic stress disorder 73% of the time

- Increase your attention span after only 4 days

- Reduce school suspensions by 45%

- Reduce stress, control anxiety, promote emotional health, enhance self-awareness, lengthen attention span, generate kindness, help fight addictions and even reduce age-related memory loss

With all these benefits (and more), one can't help but wonder why more people don't meditate. It's no longer mystic hocus pocus practiced by Tibetan Monks. The western world is beginning to reap the rewards of an ancient practice. If you're new to it, here are some basic principles to help you get started.

First, rethink how you view meditation. When I say the word "rest," you likely think it has to do with sleeping. But it's important that you learn to rest while awake. Meditation is to your mind like soap is to your hands. It's not something you do once. You have to do it every day because your mind will get contaminated with negative thoughts.

It's a myth that your mind should be blank during meditation. Technically, it's impossible for your mind to be totally blank. You're going to be thinking about something, even if it's a blank screen. The goal during meditation is for you to learn how to direct and control your thoughts, not eliminate them.

Start by taking slow, deep breaths- in through your nose, out through your mouth. Fill your lungs, release. Count them one by one. This focuses your mind on the breaths, an easy target that will help keep it from wandering.

If your mind wanders, do not pass any judgment. Remember, it's perfectly normal (especially at first).

Simply nudge your thoughts back into place.

Start small to develop the habit and be consistent with your small goal. For example, just 3-5 minutes a day, during the same time each day. Commit to 30 days in a row and reward yourself.

If you're about to go into a tough or uncomfortable conversation, give yourself the gift of one minute. Few situations are so urgent they cannot wait 30 or 60 seconds. Find a quiet space and do a quick, slow breathing meditation and notice what a difference it makes as you show up to the conversation.

Once you feel comfortable with a basic meditation, begin mixing in a vision of who you are becoming. Make it a retreat for you to visit your future self and exercise your faith as you move toward it in thought and activity. Becoming is the most powerful mindset of all. It's you in forward motion. It's even better than being because being means you've stopped. Being is where you are at this moment whereas becoming is progressing.

FUTURE SELF

How you see yourself is absolutely critical. If you're like most people, you judge yourself based on your past because that's where the evidence lies and your brain is programmed to gather the memories that support your thought. And you judge others based on their present situation because that's the supporting evidence you see before you now. Yet, neither is an accurate or fair judgment.

God sees you (and everyone else) as the person you are capable of becoming. We'll call this your future self. That's why He loves you as much as He does. That's why He never gives up on you in spite of all your faults. He simply has a different perspective of you than everyone else. He sees you for who you are becoming, not just who you are being.

What would happen if you could see yourself as He sees you? What if you could see others as He sees them? Rather than getting angry when someone offends you, what if you understood it's their present self-talking (the incomplete version) and not their real self (the person they have not yet become). It's simply their paradigm talking. How powerful would it be to live that way? How much easier would it be to forgive?

Now that we've covered your past and present, let's discuss what lies ahead. How important is your future to you? In reality, your future does not exist in time, only as a possibility in your mind. And by the time a future date arrives, it transforms into your present. So, with the future available only as imagination, why not create something beautiful?

In the world of success, coaches and mentors teach the idea of future self. They teach us to create a vivid mental picture of who we would like to become and then to focus on becoming the type of person who has those characteristics. In other words, if you want what a successful person has, you must *first become* as a successful person is. The reward is the result of your having become a new you. While our minds are trained to first see it (have) before you believe it (become), the law of success works exactly in reverse order. You must first *become*, then *do*. Only then will you *have*.

Interestingly, the religious world teaches this same principle. It's called faith. Faith is taught all through the scriptures by ancient and modern prophets and religious leaders. God asks us to move forward into the unknown with a vision of who we may become.

When you are able to gain a crystal clear vision and you embed that vision into your mind through meditation and mindfulness, your brain begins to anticipate (hope) that version of yourself and live into it (faith). Anticipation works in two directions. When you channel your anticipation toward a bad result, called *fear*. If, however, you channel it toward a good result, called *hope* (companion to faith). Both are powerful, emotional motivators and play a huge role along your journey. One pulls you forward while the other holds you back.

Whether we're talking about your "future self" in a business meeting or "faith" in a congregation, the concept of imagining your future and living into it is one of the most transformational concepts we can embrace because you are rewriting your neural circuitry to match that of the person you are becoming. It's how athletes break world records at the Olympics and ordinary leaders become great. It's the principle behind all human progress and the method by which the greatest achievements have been accomplished. Jesus famously proclaimed that it is by our faith we are healed and miracles are performed.

This is why your imagination is so important. As a kid, you don't have a problem with this. Until age 7, your brain operated primarily in Theta waves, which is a highly creative state. This is the age of imaginary friends and limitless dreams. As you grow older, your prefrontal cortex develops and your brain waves speed up to Alpha, Beta, and even Gamma where you exist in "crazy busy" mode, inundated with interruptions, distractions, and reactions. That's why adults often label themselves as not creative. Our lives become so full we don't have time for daydreaming. In fact, maybe we were even told it was bad, so our minds have become conditioned to avoid it.

Contrary to popular opinion, creativity and imagination are not gifts reserved for the elite few who won the genetic lottery. Creativity and imagination are mental muscles that can be exercised through deliberate and regular practice. But you have to start with the belief that you can develop your imagination. Once you do, you can begin to manifest a new future for yourself.

Bottom line: believe your past is perfect, live in your present, and imagine your future. If you don't have a vision for your future, you are sentenced to repeat your past.

WHAT IS YOUR MENTAL PICTURE?

There are a few principles of success most everyone will agree on. One is your ability to create a vivid mental picture in your mind of what you want and then hold it there until it becomes a reality. This is a process of envisioning your goal. In order to create your future, you must start with a clear image of exactly what that looks like. Einstein said that your imagination is a "preview of life's coming attractions." What you think about eventually comes about.

Your mind works in pictures. If I ask you to think of the home you grew up in, you will think of a picture. Maybe you see your bedroom or the old, worn-out carpet in the living room when you walk in. You might think of your old mailbox near the street. But what you didn't do is think of a bunch of words to describe your home. At our core, you're a visual thinker.

You grew up in your home. There are photos in your family album. You walked in and out of that front door a million times. That's your past, vivid, clear and without question down to the detail (at least, until your memory starts failing you). Your present is just as simple. Look around you right now and see what you see. Every detail is there to be easily observed and noted.

But your future- that doesn't exist yet. How do you "see"

that as clearly as the chair you're sitting in right now? And how do you apply this to less tangible things, like your goals? What exactly does a picture of your future look like? What does it look like when you have become that person? What imagery comes to mind when you think about where you want to be 10 years from now? How would it feel to have achieved that goal? What will you be feeling? What's the smell in the air? The noise level? Are you in front of a large audience or alone in your office? The more you can attach your mental image to your five senses the better.

Those images are much more difficult to envision because they don't exist yet. That's why so few people ever achieve the results they're capable of. It's hard work! They require the use of your imagination, a tool you may not have used since the sixth grade. This is exactly why so many never achieve what they're capable of.

Until you develop the skill of creating and holding a mental picture in your mind of the thing you want, your mind's ability to do the job it was designed to do will be watered down. Variations of this principle have been taught over and over throughout the years by some of the greatest minds the world has produced.

Your mind produces thoughts. It broadcasts signals based on what you want. Through meditation and visualization, you can paint a mental picture of the thing you want most. Your body produces emotions. Its magnetic force attracts things into your life. Both work in tandem and both require the other to be truly effective.

Creating a vivid mental image of the thing you desire most is the first part. You must then anchor those thoughts with emotion. It is not enough to merely think about your goals. Employing your brain is a good first step but you also need to get your heart involved. Head knowledge is what you learn in the classroom, but heart knowledge is from deep down where your passions are stored.

You must develop the ability to feel what it feels like to achieve your goal so vividly that when you actually achieve it, the feeling is an old friend, not a surprise. You must take advantage of the fact that your brain cannot differentiate between reality and imagination. When you begin to feel the feelings associated with you having achieved your goal, you enter a state of anticipation and your brain goes to work on answers, ideas, relationships, solutions, and resources that support this new mental picture.

This is why your HOW is not nearly as important as your WHY. Your HOW presents itself along the way when you are ready. The hardest part is getting to the state of mind and body that you're OK with, not knowing all the answers. And moving forward for as long as it takes to bring your dream to reality. It takes faith to step ahead with a clear WHY, patiently waiting for HOW to reveal itself.

Anticipation is a powerful emotion and it's directly related to your future self. It goes hand in hand with imagination. Anticipating simply means getting emotionally charged (excited) about an event that has not occurred yet. It occurs when your imagination for an event is so vivid that you live with 100% certainty the event will take place, even though there's no guarantee it will.

For example, the night before your birthday or Christmas. You were so excited it was hard to even fall asleep. For weeks, your imagination ran wild wondering what gifts you would receive. You even got in trouble at school for daydreaming about opening them. In fact, the anticipation of an event can often be more exciting than the event itself.

You'll know you have entered a state of anticipation when you can be grateful for things that haven't happened yet. Gratitude is typically associated with things that are already in existence. You're taught to be grateful for your home, your food, your body, and your material possessions. All things you already have, which makes them easy to envision. While there's nothing wrong with being thankful for present possessions, a more advanced state of mind is feeling grateful for things that do not exist yet.

Once you learn how to create the mental image and then anchor it with emotion, the natural result will be actions and habits that align for the achieving of it. It's a law that can only end in you achieving your desire. When you plant a carrot seed and give that seed plenty of soil, water, and sunlight, the only natural result will be a carrot. You don't wonder if you're going to get an ear of corn, a potato, or even a candy bar. You know you're going to get a carrot, it's just a matter of time.

Just as real is the law of the harvest that governs your life. Nurture your mental picture with emotion over a sustained period of time and the only natural result will be your mental picture becoming a reality. Operate your life from a position of anticipation and faith rather than hoping and wishing. Make the picture real, visit it often, and step forward in faith expecting the HOW to present itself along the way.

*Feel free to tear this sheet out
and color it as you listen to the
audio, available at:*
www.MakeLifeMatter.com

*Inspire others by posting finished
coloring pages with hashtag:*
#MakeLifeMatter.

WHAT AM I

BROAD-
CASTING?

#MakeLifeMatter

CHAPTER 8
The Voices in Your Head

To change your life, you have to change your lie. But how? Where are you going to learn about mastering the art of implementing new thought patterns? You're not good at it, right? Actually, you are. You're very good at it. In fact, you're an expert. Your brain is naturally wired to turn thought into a habit and you've been doing it your whole life. You may just not realize it's happening.

Your subconscious mind isn't one to wait around for you to do it intentionally, so it does it on its own, without your help or permission. A forgiveness-not-permission kind of a guy. You just need to learn to do intentionally what you're already good at doing unintentionally.

People talk about brainwashing as if it's a bad thing. Yet never in the history of the world has our society been in need of a good brainwashing. Our minds have become soiled with negative or self-limiting thoughts. Every day you wash your hands, body, face, hair, teeth...everything but your brain. So let's get started.

We've established that the thoughts you have in your mind lead to feelings, which lead to actions, habits, and ultimately your results in life. Now let's dive in and talk about those thoughts. Sentences, really. They bounce around in your head, sometimes as jumbled words. And sometimes they escape through your mouth. Have you ever surprised yourself by saying something out loud and later realized it's been a thought that finally found an escape? When the voices in your head get loud enough, you give them an external life and those around you begin to hear what you've been thinking, god or bad.

If your self-talk has not been reprogrammed, its default setting is to "Negative." One by one over the years, the sentences in your mind have shaped your character, beliefs, and mannerisms all throughout your life. But everyone has them, right? What's the harm in just one little negative thought?

To answer this, let's imagine you pulled up to a gas station to fill up. But before you replace the cap and drive off, take a small pinch of dirt and toss it in the tank. Just one little pinch. Do this every time you gas up. It won't matter, right? The question becomes: how many pinches of dirt can you put into a gas tank before the car finally stops running entirely? And what do you have to do then? Pay someone lots of money to fix it.

Granted, negative thoughts happen. Welcome to being human. But negative *thinking* is your fault because it means you've sustained and entertained your negative thoughts, giving them a home. Negative thoughts happen TO you but negative thinking happens IN you. One is an occurrence, the other is a way of life.

And how about mediocre thinking? How do you

respond when a passing stranger asks how you are doing? "Fine, thank you," "Doing well," "OK," and my personal favorite, "I'm hanging in there." Or if you're having a bad day, you might respond with a grunt!

Let me challenge your brain just a little here. Do these describe the state of mind you want? You have huge goals you want to accomplish, yet, you walk around manifesting to the world that you're just "hanging in there?" Well, let's hope you don't lose your grip!

Since your thoughts become your reality, let's make a profound change in your life with one simple challenge: sit down and spend 3 minutes to come up with a killer response to "How are you?" Dave Ramsey has a famous reply to this question. "Better than I deserve." It's humble and grateful and just different enough to make you pause when you hear it. Not only is he reprogramming his mind every time he says it, but he's also planting a new thought seed in your brain.

Every time someone asks you that question, use your new answer and see what happens. It'll take some courage but just do it. First, notice what the response does to you inside. Notice how your body responds. Notice the spark of energy or joy it brings to the person you greeted. Imagine how you may have impacted their day by simply giving them an out-of-the-box response.

Apply this new approach to other mediocre thoughts. Change "Yeah" to "*Absolutely!*" "Uh-huh" can become

"Yessir" or "Yes ma'am." And avoid "I don't know" like the plague. It's just not good in any situation. More on this one later.

Here are three classic examples of everyday negative self-talk, along with a pro tip to alter it with one micro adjustment. Whenever you catch yourself thinking one of these negative thoughts, here are some ideas on how to turn it around:

Change a word: "I have to do this" > "I choose to do this." By changing just a single word, notice how your entire mindset shifts from negative to positive. Everything in life is a choice you get to make. You don't even have to obey the law or pay your taxes (although if you don't you won't like the consequences). But thinking you "choose" to, rather than "have" to is a much happier place to be because it keeps you in control. Remember when you were young and you told your bully friends, "You're not the boss of me?" Now you get to tell your thoughts the same thing.

Add a word: "I can't do this...yet." Maybe you're your own worst enemy. Maybe you're the one who's always telling yourself you can't do something or you're not good at doing something. Adding the word "yet" to the end of that sentence changes it entirely.

Everyone has a starting point where they fail. Remember riding a bike or learning to walk? You didn't fall and quit forever. Failure was part of the process and you inherently knew that as a child. You got up and tried over and over until you got it. There was no other option. As an adult, you simply need to change your belief system to support the idea that you're a work in progress and maybe you've failed up until now but that's OK. All you have to do is keep going and you'll be walking in no time.

Delete a word: "I can't do this." Sometimes, it's just a word that needs to go. That's it. Clean and simple. One bad word that shouldn't be there. Remove it and the meaning changes entirely. While it may not sound motivational to say you merely do something. At least it's true and it's not negative. It keeps your mind open to the possibility that one day you will do it well.

There may be other ways to clean up your language. But whatever you do, don't underestimate the power of your words. Take wisdom in what my mother used to say to me, "Watch your tongue, young man!"

NOTHING BUT THE FACTS

A negative thought can be broken down by separating out the judgment from the facts surrounding it. For example, maybe you feel you are "too fat." And maybe that nagging thought just won't leave you alone. You've learned how entertaining a negative thought will only keep manifesting the very result you so despise. Every day feels like Groundhog Day- you're living life in a loop and you can't seem to get out of your own way.

Start by identifying what your dominant, nagging thought is. If you pay close attention, you'll pick it out of the crowd. It's the one wreaking all the havoc and leaving a trail of destruction behind. This may take some time. You have tens of thousands of thoughts a day and they're coming in so fast that you don't even realize they've already gone. Slow down and begin the practice of noticing your thoughts. Identify what they are and what you are trying to make them mean.

Next, boil the thought down to an obvious, neutral fact you can believe and be thankful for. For example, "I'm fat" can turn into "I have a body." The first one is a judgment based on your opinion of how you are compared to how you should be. The second thought is both neutral and indisputable.

Judgment is a slippery slope because it is based on some element of comparison of what "should" be right. Your truth vs. someone else's truth. It's defined by the experiences and belief systems of the person passing the judgment. And where did those experiences and belief systems come from? Other people. Where did those people get their judgments? You get the idea. Totally subjective, right?

Passing judgment on a thought inflates it and gives it an emotional charge (typically a negative emotion). This charge empowers it and feeds it, giving it a position of authority in your mind. Instead, remove the judgment, bring it back down to a cold, hard fact. Its influence in your life weakens and it builds a framework from which you can start building new thought habits. For example, the next step in the evolution of that thought may be, "I have a body that serves me."

EXTERNAL VOICES

Our world is full of harmful addictions. We turn to drugs, alcohol, pornography, or even food when we want to buffer ourselves from our world. But there's one addiction more widespread and detrimental than them all: the addiction to what other people think of you. When you listen to the voices of others, you'll get thousands of different responses. Some of them are passionate, convincing, and enticing. Everyone in the world has an opinion. And there is no shortage of people anxious to share it because the human brain wants to be validated. It craves authority.

There's nothing that will hold you back more than trying to make everyone happy. Look at anyone who has achieved any level of success and you'll find a tribe of haters. Trying to please everyone requires that you stay safely inside your comfort zone where nothing great happens. Ironically, you join the ranks of those you will not make happy.

Close behind, "why?" is the second most common question in the world: what do you think? How often do you find yourself asking someone else, who may or may not even be a subject matter expert? Asking for other people's opinions is possibly the most widespread addiction in the world. And the reason is that your brain craves validation and approval, even if you have to seek the outside sources of those who are NOT subject matter experts. Besides, if you do what someone else suggested and you fail, it's their fault, not yours, right? Pressure's off.

The best advice I have found along these lines was offered by Gary Vaynerchuk during a podcast interview. He suggested pretending nobody in the world exists and learning to listen to yourself. You may make some mistakes at first, but that's how you learn. If you always seek the opinions of others, you allow those decision-making muscles in your brain to deteriorate, reinforcing your dependency on others to make decisions for you. You place the power of choice in their hands.

Imagine being a sports player as you enter the field without a home-court advantage. As you step out, you know that the majority of spectators and fans want you to lose. Crowds of wild, half-drunk, face-painted, emotionally charged fans are celebrating your failure with wiggly foam distractions. And they're happy to pay handsomely for the privilege of doing it.

As you walk out on that court or field, you have two choices: listen to the voices or tune them out. Nobody is surprised by negative fans and nobody expects the crowd to be chivalrous. "Excuse me, Mr. Ref. But could I have a moment of your time for a few suggestions?" said no one ever.

So you step up to the plate, the free-throw line...whatever it is. This is your moment. You can either focus on executing the play as you've practiced or you can focus on the crowd who is trying desperately to get you off your game. Unless your mind is strong enough, the crowd will win the day. "The crowd" wants nothing more than to be the reason you didn't succeed. The crowd rejoices in your failure.

Can you imagine a professional athlete taking suggestions from the sidelines? "Sorry, sir- could you say that again? I couldn't quite hear you. Do I need to swing a little higher? You mean, like this?"

In the sports world, if you buy a ticket, you can come to the game. Nobody scrutinizes your expertise. You're free to bring your signs, your face paint, and your loud opinions. You are free to bark orders to professional athletes about a game you yourself may have never coached or even played before. So if you're going to sign a contract for millions of dollars a year for the privilege of doing something you love, you had better be able to handle the criticism. It's part of the game.

It's no different in the game of life. Why do we expect the world to just "see" what we see and support us in our vision and passion? Of course, they won't. When we begin stepping out in the direction of our dreams, why would we expect to not get critics, many of whom have never stepped out themselves? They're seated comfortably on the sidelines where there's no risk, plenty of beer, and giant foam fingers. When you take a stand and move your life in a new direction, there are those who are silently afraid of losing you because you are becoming a new version of yourself. You are moving ahead but they are not. So they try to hold you back to avoid losing you. Tragically, it works all too often.

There will always be plenty of voices that do not matter. White noise. Tune them out just as an NBA player does, standing on the free-throw line. It's you who has the loudest and most influential voice in your world. That's one of your most powerful weapons. You can drown out a crowd of ten thousand external voices by simply raising your one internal voice. This is why successful people talk to themselves. Self-talk doesn't mean someone is going crazy. Self-talk means someone is so much in touch with their inner voice that a burning desire has pulled the monolog from deep within your core up to the surface.

Other people are always anxious to share their truth, also known as an opinion. If you allow your mind to be filled with other people's opinions, you'll never have room for your own truth to take root. You'll always be subject to what other people think. And with over seven billion different opinions in this world, is that a life you want to live?

Every time anyone steps out in the direction of their dreams, naysayers come out of the woodwork to tear that person down, like crabs in a bucket. But you don't have to allow it to mean anything to you. When they show up, expect them and respond neutrally in your mind. "Oh, there you are, right on schedule. Wish I had time to stay and chat but I have more important things to do, so have a great day."

If you're still learning how to control the voices in your head, you're in good company. I have yet to find a school that offers *Thinking 101* as a class (although, based on the state of our world, it might not be a bad idea). The truth is, most of us were never taught how to handle, manage or direct our thoughts. Unless you take the time to learn, you may never discover who you truly are or what you are capable of.

STATE OF THE YOUNION

Every year, we get to hear our president talk about the state of our Union. And while some speeches are more compelling than others, the idea is that we all participate in an overview of what's been going on and a grand vision for what lies ahead. What if you did the same thing for your life? What is the state of your union?

If you take a road trip across the country, you'll see road signs welcoming you each time you enter a new state. Some states are large and you'll drive for hours in long stretches of open road. Other states are small and crowded with heavily populated cities. As you make the journey through life, you'll be sure to enter different states of mind as well. Some are quite pleasant and welcoming- you might just spend a night or two. Others don't suit you well. Maybe they feel old, dirty, and run down. And some states of mind are simply destructive places to stay.

Here are a few of the worst states of mind that are sure to come knocking at your mind's door. Give each a name and recognize it when it comes. "Oh, Fred! You're back, huh? No surprise there. But do you *really* think you're going to get to me this time?"

1. FEAR

Fear is not what it used to be. We're not running from saber-toothed tigers anymore or wooly mammoth stampedes. In today's modern era, fear occurs while worrying about what *might* happen, but will likely NOT happen. Think about that sentence. So many of us spend time and energy worrying about something that has not happened yet but *might* happen. Of all the powerful things you can do with your thoughts, worrying is at the bottom of the list. It means using your precious imagination to *rehearse* the worst-case scenario. Guess what's more likely to happen?

Granted, you didn't always respond this way, you learned to fear things. As a baby, you weren't afraid of anything. Adults around you taught you about fear when you reached for a hot stove or a sharp object and they freaked out. When a snake slithered by or a spider crawled up the wall, you learned fear by observing the reactions of others. Since your fears were all learned, they can also be unlearned.

The best way to eliminate fear is to face it head-on. 99 times out of 100, you'll find it's nowhere near the size of the monster you thought it was. In fact, it's likely just a timid little mouse. Pick a fear and break it down to one simple action you can take. If you have a fear of snakes, start by reading a nature book about snakes. If you're terrified of public speaking, host a Facebook live video. Eliminate fear by doing the very thing you fear.

Another way to dissolve fear is to associate it with something silly or ridiculous. Imagine that snake wearing a ball cap, coiled up and bouncing around like Tigger as it chases a ball. Dissociating the fear from what makes it scary convinces your mind that the thing you fear also has a funny side. It's not 100% scary after all.

2. NEGATIVITY

There's a difference between negativity and negative thoughts. A negative thought can pop in unannounced at any time. It needs no invitation. It's natural for you to think of negative thoughts unintentionally from time to time.

But when negative thoughts become a habit, it's called negativity. One is something that happens to you while the other is something that becomes you. Once a negative thought seed is given the opportunity to sprout roots, it will take over your beautiful garden. And one day you become that person. You know the one: the guy who's always pointing out what's wrong about something.

Have you ever noticed how negative-minded people tend to spend time together? Maybe you've been sucked into a conversation around the water cooler at work. The latest juicy gossip is just too much to resist. 20 minutes later, you're back at your desk and you have an unsettled feeling. You can't focus, you've just lost your mojo. Maybe you heard something about someone and now you see them differently. Maybe a new fear was planted in your brain. You carry it home and get impatient with your children or pets. One negative conversation or thought can plant a seed that results in a spiral of negativity. It can also zap your energy.

The news media has the same effect. They don't get paid to tell positive stories because people don't click on happy headlines. It's the steamy pile of manure that attracts the most flies. The more you're exposed to negativity, the more it affects your mind. No matter how strong you think you are, prolonged exposure will take its toll. Developing a positive state of mind takes intentional, consistent practice. It's not easy- you need all the help you can get.

The key to eliminating negative thinking is to become aware and then correct yourself. Remember in high school when you were scrambling for a decent grade and you asked our teacher for any makeup work or redo's you could do? Take advantage of the fact that you now get as many redos as you like. For example, when something goes wrong and you hear yourself ask, "Why me?", reframe the question. "What's right about this?" or, "What am I supposed to learn here?"

Everything that happens to you has the potential to be positive or negative. Circumstances all start out neutral. It's not until you assign it meaning that it becomes good or bad. That makes it 100% within your control. You're already an expert at assigning meaning— you've been doing it your whole life. All you need to do is first become aware that you're in control and start intentionally assigning a meaning that will serve you better.

3. DOUBT

Doubt is the opposite of faith. Doubt suggests you are unsure of your future rather than being excited by it. It's one of the biggest stealers of dreams in this life because the Universe does not reward fence-sitters.

How many times have you made a decision and then second-guessed your decision because of something someone said? Even a complete stranger! If you're too easily swayed by the random comments of others, you will never achieve anything worthwhile. Doubting your own decisions keeps you in the foggy, lukewarm middle.

There's nothing wrong with being open to the expertise of others. In fact, we were all raised by a village. Of course, you need to seek ideas, thoughts, and solutions outside of your bubble. But unless you know that a person is qualified to speak on the subject, what they share is nothing more than an opinion. Be careful which of them you allow into your sphere of influence or you'll doubt your way back into a safe, comfortable space where greatness and opportunity do not hang out.

Uncertainty is built into this thing we call life. Nobody knows if they have tomorrow. Nobody is guaranteed anything. We all have to get used to the fact that at any time, your life could change permanently, for the worse. As a life insurance agent, I have these types of conversations with people regularly. A life insurance policy doesn't protect the policyholder from death. It protects loved ones from financial ruin. We talk about the worst that can happen and then take action to minimize the consequences by writing an insurance policy. When someone buys a life insurance policy, they're buying peace of mind. They are eliminating one layer of fear from their lives. One less thing to worry about.

Guess what? You can do the same. Accepting the idea that life is uncertain will help dispel fear, resulting in a higher level of self-confidence. Prepare for the worst-case scenario and you raise your level of self-confidence a notch. You feel less inclined to adjust your sails every time doubt creeps in and more inclined to stay the course you've picked. Confidence is a thing you do, not a thing you feel. It means taking action in spite of self-doubt and limiting beliefs, not in the absence of them. Become confident by choosing to be confident, even when you don't "feel" like it.

Carefully select your field of influence, as you would a job candidate. Program your mind to the idea that you are your own best friend. Starting now, nobody treats you as well as you do. And when you have a passion, a hunch, an intuition, it's every bit as valid as the world's foremost expert on the subject. The more you trust yourself, the more you'll discover you are worth trusting.

4. INDECISION

Doubt and indecision are twin troublemakers. Where there's doubt, indecision is not far behind. When you doubt yourself, the last thing you want to do is make a decision because you stand a good chance at being wrong, and nobody likes to be wrong. So, why would you want the risk? Instead, why not stay safely in the realm of indecision where you can still hang on to some level of dignity? Not making a decision means you do not have to be wrong and you get to remain on your impossible path toward perfectionism.

Suppose I asked you to grab a cup of sugar in the pantry. When you open the door you notice two identical bins. One contains flour, the other is full of sugar. You don't know which is which. You think of how delicious the cookies will be when they're done. But right now, everything lies on your shoulders. Choose wrong and you ruin the entire batch.

This is your moment (queue the theme music). BUT... what if you choose wrong? Your heart starts pounding. What if you open one bin and it's NOT sugar. What then? What if people laugh at you and call you crazy? Maybe it's better to just stall and change the subject. Anything to avoid being wrong.

I agree it's a dramatized example. But in principle, it's no different from the majority of decisions you make (or don't make) every day. Ironically, you will not learn until you make a decision. Yet, you want to be right so badly that you avoid the risk of making a wrong decision. So you stay stuck in the safe space of your comfort zone and forfeit the glory of progress that can only come from risking a wrong decision. How does any of that make sense?

Let's go back to our silly example. Here's how it would likely play out. Without a second thought, you choose a lid and open it. You look inside. If it's not sugar, you simply close the lid and open the other one. If it is sugar, you got it right the first time and saved a little time and effort. Either way, you'll come back with the sugar and you'll eat the cookies. You don't worry about making the wrong choice. You know it's a possibility but you also know it's not going to change the outcome. You'll either learn which is the right bin or you'll learn which is not. Both are valuable answers.

What if you took this same approach in other areas of your life? Quickly weigh out the pros and cons, and go with what your gut says. Course correct if it was the wrong choice. No emotional drama. No shame or fear. Just small, simple course corrections.

Far too often we overthink a decision and talk ourselves out of it because we don't have all the information. But guess how many people make decisions without all the knowledge? Nearly everyone. Why would you expect anything different? Of course, you're not going to have all the answers. Answers often come after making a decision. You only need enough information to light up your spidey senses and have a hunch. And the faster you pick something the sooner you'll know if it was right or not.

The most successful people I know are quick decision-makers. The next time you and your friends start that old familiar conversation, "what do you want to do tonight?" "I don't know, what do you want to do?" Be the one that breaks the cycle. Make a decision and suggest something.

Each decision you make will either be right or it will be a lesson. Either way, you win. See life that way and you will never be a failure. You learn by doing. That's why the HOW cannot easily be taught. How everyone achieves their dream is unique to them. You will learn your way just as they did: by doing and pivoting. Make decisions quickly, learn, adjust and keep going. If it turns out to be the wrong decision, rather than burden your mind with guilt and shame, simply put the lid back on the bin and open the other one.

5. VICTIMHOOD

What are some of the excuses you've allowed to stop you from progressing in your life? Maybe you're too old? Too young? Maybe you're not educated enough or lack experience. "Who's going to listen to a newbie like me when the market is saturated with gurus?" You may have grown up in a single-parent home on the brink of poverty. Maybe your health isn't ideal. Or perhaps your home wasn't in the right state or country. Your neighbors were weirdos. Your friends at school made fun of you and it's their fault.

All of these problems have one thing in common: you are the victim and something or someone else is to blame for your troubles.

In this world of convenience, information, and technology, it's easy to develop a victim mentality. In fact, the victim mentality will prevail unless you intentionally develop a mindset to counteract it.

Today's social media feeds are filled with perfect photos of all your friends (most of whom you've never met) living the good life. Beaches, vacations, hanging out at clubs and bars with friends. What's wrong with you? Your life looks much different. You have a messy house, stress at work and your toddler has a poopy diaper. You don't even have time to get your nails done. Something is "wrong" with your life. Everyone else has somehow figured it out and you've been left out in the lurch.

Every excuse you feel is 100% legitimate has been overcome by thousands of others who succeeded under the same or worse circumstances. Rather than choosing a *victim* mentality, they shifted to a *victor* mentality, seeing circumstances as what they are: neutral until they are assigned a meaning. And who's in charge of making that assignment? You. This means your circumstances are either the obstacles that keep you from achieving results or the reasons you do achieve them.

Here's a truth that may sting just a little: you are exactly where you are today because of you and you alone.

I'm sure you can make a list a mile long of reasons why this statement is not true and does not apply to your life. Even if you were right, believing that way will only continue to inhibit your ability to move forward. It will never serve you well in your life to think that way. So whether it's true or not, what value do you get to continue believing it?

Instead, own your past. It frees you up so you can move forward into a better future. Remember that circumstances are neutral, waiting for you to assign meaning to them. Make them mean something that will serve you. Be thankful for your past, for it has gotten you to exactly this point in time in your life. What a blessing that is! Now that you are here at this moment you can confidently move forward with a knowledge of what NOT to do. Today will mark a major changing point in your life for the better. And isn't that something to be thankful for?

Keep yourself protected from the harmful influence of the masses. Don't allow the noise to stop you from your dreams. Build confidence in yourself and your vision by looking inward to self and upward to God. Celebrate your wins along the way and anticipate a beautiful future. It's your life to live. You've got one shot and nobody else can or will ever live it for you. God gave it to you and you alone.

Make your life matter!

*Feel free to tear this sheet out
and color it as you listen to the
audio, available at:*
www.MakeLifeMatter.com

*Inspire others by posting finished
coloring pages with hashtag:*
#MakeLifeMatter.

CHAPTER 9

12 Steps to Make Your Life Matter

We now have a solid foundation about what it takes to make your life matter. Let's review by boiling everything down to a series of essential steps. The first five steps are your foundation. That's nearly half of the entire process, which is a good indication of how important your foundation is. Without it, your building will crumble, no matter how good your blueprints are.

1. DEVELOP A BURNING DESIRE

The first step is desire. Nothing happens unless your heart yearns for it. "Desire" is an interesting word. You can't "kind of" desire something. It's an all-or-nothing kind of a thing. There are too many forces already working against you to expect to succeed without it. Success is an uphill battle and you need all the allies you can get. Desire is like a whole army of soldiers on your side.

What do you want most? What lights you up and where do you have a burning desire to succeed? Why do you want it and how much does it mean to you?

Finding a burning desire is simple. It's always ignited just as soon as you discover your passion. The two go hand in hand.

In his book Think and Grow Rich, Napoleon Hill brilliantly summed it up this way: "Any dominating idea, plan or purpose held in the mind, through repetition of thought, and emotionalized with a Burning Desire for its realization, is TAKEN OVER by the subconscious part of the mind and acted upon, and it is thus carried through to its logical climax by whatever natural means may be available."

Our society is programmed to churn out lukewarm worker bees. Well-intentioned people who started out with bright hopes are now dimmed by the fog of the daily grind and a leaky passion tank. We enter a school system that grades us based on our ability to memorize answers short-term. High school teaches us math, science, and grammar, but there are no classes for finances, stress management or discovering your life's passion. By the time we're done with college, we are burdened with massive amounts of debt and no clear path. After all, who has time to chase their passion when there are bills to pay?

Many "fall" into whatever job they can get and simply stay there until they retire, serving time like a prison sentence. 10 years in, maybe you paused and looked around. "Is this what I signed up for?" "Is this what I dreamed of when I was a child?" What happened?

"Well, it's too late now. Guess I'll just finish out my term since this is all I know how to do anyway." Sound familiar?

Regardless of how old or young you are, take some of your free time to discover yourself and notice what gets you so excited you can't stop thinking about it. Maybe you think there isn't anything. That you're the one odd man who doesn't have a burning desire for something. To that I say, it's out there- you just haven't found it yet. I have a tool to help you do this! Download the free LifePlan document at **MakeLifeMatter.com**.

2. PAINT A CLEAR MENTAL PICTURE

Once you truly desire something, you need to become an artist. Pick up a brush and paint a new picture of the person you must become in order to achieve your desired outcome. Everything in life is about becoming, not the gold medal (AKA shiny object) that hangs around your neck at the finish line (although gold medals are kind of nice).

To paint a new picture, you have to use something you may not have used since kindergarten: your imagination. A good way to define imagination is simply a memory of your future. Remember when you had imaginary friends? You have the skill, you may just be out of practice. Like riding a bike, you can learn it all over again.

Envisioning is a skill eventually mastered by all the top athletes and performers in the world. Jack Nicklaus understood this concept. "I never hit a shot, not even in practice, without having a very sharp in-focus picture of it in my head. It's like a color movie. First I "see" where I want it to finish, nice and white and sitting high on the bright green grass. Then the scene quickly changes, and I "see" the ball going there: its path, trajectory, and shape, even its behavior on landing. Then there's a sort of fade-out, and the next scene shows me making the kind of swing that will turn the previous images into reality."

Be like Jack and envision your future in vivid color. The more vivid you paint your picture, the better the clarity you will have.

Practice holding that mental picture in your mind. You'll be terrible at it when you first begin. Try holding the picture for 10 seconds, then 20. Use meditation and visualization techniques to strengthen your mind's ability to hold a thought for an extended period of time. What you're doing is training your most valuable asset to start working for you rather than against you.

Once you are good at visualizing, start to emotionally connect with that new picture on a daily basis. Repeated thoughts become beliefs but anchoring those thoughts with emotion accelerates the process exponentially by creating coherence between heart and mind. Dr. Joe Dispenza is a brilliant teacher of heart/mind coherence. You would do well to study his work.

Take it one step further by practicing future gratitude. Express thanks for the desired outcome, even though it hasn't happened yet. That will mess with your mind just a little. Being grateful for events that haven't happened yet requires faith, but as you practice anticipation, gratitude will become the natural outcome.

If you need help, you can download the free meditation tools at **MakeLifeMatter.com**.

3. BUILD YOUR CIRCLE OF INFLUENCE

We've all heard that you become like the five people you spend the most time with. Guess what? It's you who gets to choose who those five influences are. If you're not intentional about building your core circle of influence, society will choose them for you. How comfortable are you with that? Either way, there will be a handful of people who heavily influence your life, whether you like it or not. So you might as well craft that team with intention and care.

If you're around a winning circle of leaders, you're putting the odds in your favor that they will bring you along. If your circle of influence is negative, it'll be almost impossible to reach your burning desire.

Build your circle one at a time. Find someone who IS where you want to be and take him or her out to lunch. Explain your situation, ask for advice and become accountable. Keep in mind, a mentor is not someone you admire. A mentor is someone whose advice you follow.

If your mentor is no longer alive, invest time by absorbing their works through books, audios, etc.

Success leaves clues and you are Sherlock Holmes. In fact, you can appoint a full board of directors of your own and "hang out" with whomever you want. Get to know them so well that you can imagine the advice they'd give you. You become like those you spend the most time with, so choose wisely.

There's a second side to this step. You must also give back by becoming a mentor by teaching others. It's been said that you haven't truly learned something until you are able to teach it to someone else in a way that's easy for them to understand. The best way to learn something is to teach it.

As you grow and learn from someone who is where you want to be, pay it forward because however far along your journey you are, it's exactly where someone else wants to be. It's not only about giving of yourself and serving others but it's also about helping you solidify what you're learning yourself. The best way to learn something is to teach it.

4. CLEAN UP YOUR ENVIRONMENTS

You have four environments that affect everything you do: physical, mental, virtual, and social. The amount of willpower you have to pursue your purpose is limited. So, stack your environment in your favor by removing the stops. We just talked about one of them: your social environment. These are the people you spend the most time with. Make sure they will bring you along in the right direction. You are much more likely to fail at losing 10 pounds when your pantry shelves are stocked with sugary treats. So why make it hard on yourself? Out of sight, out of mind, out of body.

But you have three other environments that are also critical. Take time and dive into each one. Look closely at what you have in your environment that may inhibit your ability to move toward your vision of your future.

Organize your office (physical) and throw out all those piles you're never going to do anything with or that old Christmas gift you feel guilty throwing out. It's just stuff. It's liberating to free yourself of the burden of it.

Clean up your thoughts (mental) by paying attention to the little ones that fly under the radar. Starting with your very first thought of the day. When something goes wrong, do you still look for what's right about it? Mental toughness is not easy, that's why many people never achieve it. Become obsessed with positive inputs and repulsed by negative ones. Thoughts are rarely facts or truth. You aren't required to think a thought just because it's a fact. When it comes to thought, you decide what you keep and what you discard. What you keep will become "you truth."

Proactively unfollow any post or person that is not in alignment with your purpose and mission from step 2 (virtual). Clean up your feed. Social media should nourish you rather than make you feel guilty, afraid, or ashamed. Subscribe to good news and positive thoughts and block out negative news and "friends." Train your virtual environment to become an asset for you.

Never stop paying attention to your environments. Your willpower isn't strong enough to get you there on its own.

5. MIND YOUR MONOLOGUE

Remember that little kid in your 3rd-grade class who talked to himself? Guess what? He was on to something. Folks might think your crazy, but there's power in using a self monologue.

Mama always told you to mind your manners, right? Even more important is managing the space between your ears and using your voice to speak things into existence. Orphaned thoughts are constantly roaming around looking for a place to call home. Every parasite needs a host. As soon as you start thinking something negative or limiting, you can easily replace it right away by speaking a new thought into existence. Your inner voice can drown out a thousand outer voices.

Never let anything come out of your mouth you do not want to come true in your life. The law of attraction is more powerful than you think. Thoughts, words, actions. Those are your building blocks.

Start speaking what you want and don't be afraid of being alone with yourself. You're a freaking miracle! Become your own biggest fan- a constant force for good in your own life.

6. TAKE MASSIVE ACTION

With your foundation in place, it's time to DO something. If you don't know what to do, take the next best step with the information and resources you have available to you at this time. But whatever you do, do NOT do nothing. Remember the flour/sugar story? The sooner you pick something the sooner you'll know what to do (or what not to do). Both are valuable. Worry less about what decision to make and more about course-correcting after making a decision.

As you take action, back it with faith that the road ahead of you will be revealed as you go, but only if you're in motion. God cannot steer a parked car.

Every action toward your desire, regardless of how small, will build your self-confidence. Once you start keeping your own commitments, you will love yourself more and gain a higher self-value and self-worth. The more you love yourself, the less you care about what other people think of you, ultimately leading to the confidence you need to take more action.

Solid self-confidence only comes after breaking the worst addiction in the world: seeking the approval of others. If you're a chronic approval seeker, get honest with yourself, acknowledge it, and start retraining your brain to change it, using the steps and principles taught in this book.

If you struggle taking action, start small- put something on your calendar and do it. Keep daily commitments to yourself. Fail quickly!

Finally, act as if what you want already exists because it does. This is the step that requires you to move forward without knowing exactly what to expect. Trust in God, the Universe, or whatever kind of Higher Power you choose. But believe that some power exists out there that wants you to achieve your goals and become the best version of yourself you can. Hang onto that belief and act as if you already were that person.

A good question to ask yourself is, "What would the future me do in this situation?" The clearer your mental picture the clearer your answers will come. But answers are much easier than action. Nothing replaces massive action. Hustle beats talent 9 times out of 10.

If you're a chronic overthinker, start forcing yourself to make decisions and take action before you think you are ready. It may intimidate you a little at first, which is a sign you're headed in the right direction. Ready, fire, aim.

7. ESTABLISH ROUTINES & HABITS

Successful people understand that you make your own habits, but then your habits make you. And a routine is nothing more than a cluster of habits. Whether you care to admit it or not, we are creatures of habit and routine. It helps us make sense of our world by providing predictability and familiarity. It can work in your favor, provided your habits support your direction in life. But make no mistake, your habits will either make you or break you.

There's a lot of talk about willpower. We love to say things like, "where there's a will there's a way," putting willpower in the spotlight. And while there's certainly a place for it, you cannot become who you want to be on willpower alone (conscious mind). Willpower is of limited supply and slowly depletes as you go through the day like a bucket with a hole in it. That's why good sleep is so important- you need to replenish your supply.

In order to get to the root of why you do what you do every day, you have to get down to a much deeper place than willpower can go. It's in your subconscious world where habits truly run the show. A physical habit can take 3 weeks to develop but a mental habit can take much longer, depending on how prepared your brain is to accept and change it. So, commit to the long haul.

There are certain habits you will need to develop in order to achieve your vision or goal. If you know what those are, make a plan to knock them out one by one. If you don't know what habits you will need, begin with the habit of studying. Select a mentor and begin to study their teachings regularly. From there, you'll learn exactly what else you need to do. Remember, as soon as you get in motion, the answers will come.

To help you with this, I recommend using Mattercards. I also have several free meditations you can download on **MakeLifeMatter.com**. You'll also find suggestions on morning and evening routines.

8. STAY IN YOUR LANE

Would you like to know how to pick the fastest lane at the grocery store every single time? First step: pick a lane (any lane). Second step: don't look at any other lane.

The only reason you're frustrated at how slow your lane is going is that you looked to the left and right and noticed they're going faster. It's the awareness of the circumstance that creates frustration. Before you knew the other lane was going faster, you were happy. The key is to NOT notice because all the frustration comes from the knowledge. In this case, ignorance truly is bliss.

You cannot control how fast the cashiers move, how fast people swipe their cards, what items need to be looked up or taken back. There are a hundred situations that can cause delays. Since all one hundred of them are out of your control, you must learn to let them go and focus, instead, on what you can control: your thoughts and what's in front of you at this moment. Besides, striking up a meaningful conversation with that stranger standing in front of you may end up being the highlight of your day.

Comparison is the biggest thief of confidence. It's not fair to yourself. Think about it. Because you know yourself inside and out, you get to become intimately familiar with all your own insecurities, failures, doubts, and fears. After all, you've been with yourself through thick and thin your entire life. Am I wrong?

Compare that to what you think when you see others, who primarily talk about their successes and victories. Essentially, you're comparing your bloopers reel to someone else's highlights reel. "What's wrong with me?" "Why does my life not look like that?" "How come everything comes so easily to her?" "Why is it taking so long to scan a bag of cantaloupes?"

In reality, everyone has victories and everyone has challenges. You just don't get to see all of them. You get to see what they want you to see, so it's already an unfair comparison from the beginning. Every minute you spend comparing yourself to others is 60 seconds of wasted time you'll never get back. It serves zero value and zero purpose in your life. A wise man once said that the only person you should compare yourself to is you yesterday. Stay in your own lane and watch your confidence blossom.

9. RELABEL AND REPROGRAM

Use the free tools at **MakeLifeMatter.com** to develop your life foundation and clarify your vision. Then, remind your brain every day of this new image of yourself. This can be one of the most difficult steps because life gets noisy. Ever met anyone who isn't "crazy busy" with something?

Just like the "pay yourself first" concept that applies to money, pay yourself first with time. Give yourself the first few precious moments of each day with mindfulness, meditation, and focus. Practice gaining clarity on that new mental image you painted of yourself in step 2. Just like focusing a microscope on a blob of bacteria, gaining clarity on your vision will take micro-adjusting and practice.

Direct your thoughts on what will be the most important or meaningful things you can do with your day. Make it part of your morning routine to envision yourself winning. If you don't have time in the mornings, wake up earlier. These are your dreams we're talking about! Of course, they require sacrifice.

Write down your vision every day on your Mattercard and use it during meditation to envision it with as much clarity as you can muster up. Every day? Yes! Every. Single. Day. Meditation is like bathing- you need to do it every day.

How bad do you want it? If you don't want something bad enough to write it down every day, revisit step one and double-check your desire for the goal. A weak desire won't be enough to feed the fire that will push you through the storms that lie ahead.

Writing down and reviewing your vision every day strengthens the mental muscle and sharpens your focus for that thing. It also helps provide blinders to distractions, negativity, and noise. Essentially, you're hacking into your mind and reprogramming it to operate like the type of person who has what you want.

Only, it's 100% legal.

10. EXPECT URGES

Getting yourself to a new version of yourself requires stepping out and accepting more risk. It's your brain's job to keep you safe, so don't be surprised when your brain tries to stop you with an urge.

Your past will pop up inside your head on a daily basis. But the last thing you want to do is resist. You have to be OK with it as a natural part of your journey. Have you ever tried to push a ball down below the water's surface? How far can you go before it pops back up? The further down you push, the hard it gets to keep it from bursting up to the surface. There's a great lesson there.

Instead, expect it and accept it. Redirect, but don't resist. When you go "third party" in your mind, you can politely say to the urge, "Duly noted. I appreciate your opinion. Please sit back down because I'm in charge around here."

Just like that, there's a new Sheriff in town.

11. CELEBRATE PROGRESS

Our world offers far too little praise. As much as you may say you don't need it, if you're human, you absolutely do. And you're just the one to give it to yourself because nobody else knows how much progress you're making. Capture your wins and take a moment at the end of each day to write one down. Pause to mentally pat yourself on your back.

If you make this a daily habit (which I strongly recommend), the day will come where you'll have to really start thinking hard to think of a win. This is where your habit will be put to the test. "I didn't really do anything noteworthy today." Oops- that's the start of a bad thought habit creeping in.

Remember, you're a walking talking miracle. You're God's greatest creation. Surely there's at least one single win you could celebrate. One of the great challenges of our age is that modern technology has made the marvelous mundane. Anything that is less than spectacular hardly gets noticed. What would be a miracle to someone 50 years ago is taken for granted today.

To counteract this, you'll have to get good at noticing the small, seemingly insignificant wins that happen around you or because of you. But make no mistake, they are there if you look for them. So, release those little endorphins! You've earned it and you need it.

12. COMMIT TO NEVER QUIT

Do NOT doubt yourself ever again. You are too valuable. You truly are an absolute walking, talking miracle. Doubt and fear are the biggest barriers to success ever. Doubting yourself means comparing yourself today to a small-minded version of yourself from yesterday.

Why would you do that to yourself? It means you don't believe you can grow or learn new things. You've proven all throughout your life that's not true. Otherwise, you'd still be crawling around on the floor. Rather than doubting yourself, why not recognize how far you've come and believe you can go further, even if it's just a few steps for now.

One final note: there is one element in all of this that nobody can predict: your timeline.

Bob Proctor has taught us that we can know the exact gestation period of a carrot. We know how long it will take a flower to bloom. We can even predict with a great deal of accuracy the due date of a pregnant human being. But nobody knows the gestation period of your dream. That's the part that requires faith. That's the one element God put into the equation to keep Him part of your journey.

You have control over developing a desire, painting a clear picture, and finding a mentor. You can 100% clean up your environment and your mental monologue, although that one may take some serious effort. It's up to you to take massive action, establish routines and stay focused. And, it's completely within your control to relabel, expect urges, celebrate success, and not quit.

But you simply cannot predict how long you must do all these things before your vision transfers itself from imagination to real life.

Many of us are able to do the right things for a period of time. A day, a week, a month, even maybe a year. But here's the question that separates the men from the boys: can you keep doing these things for a sustained period of time? Can you do the hard things as long as it takes? Can you hang on?

"How long?" you might ask. There is only one answer: as long as it takes. That's the best answer anyone can give you. Not only do you have to stay on track, try, fail, recommit, get dirty, fail again, nearly quit, dust yourself off, bang your head against the wall, and a host of other bumps and bruises, but in spite of it all, you must not quit and you must keep doing it until you achieve your dream.

For some, the gestation period may be measured in months. We see their stories and all long to have overnight success as they have. For most, it's measured in years, sometimes decades. But regardless of how long it will take, one thing you can be assured of: success will come. It cannot NOT come. The law of the harvest is not respecter of persons. It doesn't care about your line of work, special talents, genes or what you've done in your past. If you sow the seeds and nourish them, plants will sprout and the tree will bear fruit. It's as much a law of success as it is a law that governs gardening.

So enjoy the journey because as long as you're on track, you simply need to stay there. Your success is inevitable. So you might as well enjoy yourself rather than putting off your happiness to the finish line.

One final note about these 12 steps. It's cyclical, not linear. There is no endpoint. Developing a burning desire isn't something you do once and check off your list. Nor is step 12 the place you end up. There is no beginning and no end. You're always in process, always on your journey. Your goals change, your needs change and your dreams, desires, and values constantly evolve throughout your life. You may enter this cycle on step 5 or step 10, it doesn't matter. Know what's in front of you and what to expect. You're in this for the long haul.

I hope by now this book is messy, full of sticky tabs, highlights, underlines, scribbles and notes. Some of it may be from the words on the page that have inspired you. But do not discount the ideas that will come to you as a result of reading. Both are relevant.

It's not enough to read and say, "oh, that's nice." In order for any of this to work, you have to take action. This is self-help, not shelf help.

You have one life to live,
make it matter!

Getting Debt-Free is Much Closer Than You Think

One of the most debilitating and draining things in life is debt. Debt says you don't own something (and it likes to rub that in). Even worse, it can mean you haven't owned a certain habit from your past and now you bear a burden that binds you down with that constant, nagging voice of regret.

What if all you needed to do was adjust the way you're doing things?

If there was a way to get out of debt faster, not spend any more money than you already are and end up with a large amount when you do, would you want to know about it?

It costs you nothing to find out:

Your Golden Years Start Today

There are few things in life that are tax free. Life insurance is one of them. And when designed properly, you can use life insurance for a tax-free, lifetime retirement income. It's like purchasing your own pension plan...minus the partnership with Uncle Sam.

If you're concerned that social security may not be enough, or you like the idea of taking taxes out of the equation, reach out to our office. We have products that grow based on the performance of an index, but will not lose money when the market crashes.

If you really want to blow your mind, have us run an illustration on one of your kids or grandkids and watch the eighth wonder of the world in action.

Schedule a conversation here:

How's That Nest Egg?

You've worked hard at building up your 401K. What if another market crash happens? What if your 401K turns into a 201K or even a Special K? Can you risk losing your retirement?

The market cycles. It always has. It's going to drop again, it always does. The trouble is, nobody knows when.

Would you feel better safeguarding your hard-earned savings into a plan with nice, steady growth that is guaranteed NOT to lose, and guaranteed to pay you for the rest of your life, even when your funds dry up?

If you got chills just now, schedule a chat with us:

It's 10pm.
Do you Know Where
Your Policy Is?

Most people take one of the most important documents of their life and stick it in a cabinet drawer where it doesn't see the light of day for years. Without looking, can you describe with 100% accuracy the terms and benefits of your life insurance policy?

Don't wait until someone dies to find out what you have. Our team would consider it an honor to help you dust off that bad boy and review it with you. It will cost you nothing except 15 minutes of your time. We'll answer questions and make sure you're getting the best rates and coverage available.

Schedule your free policy review here:

This Ain't Your Grandpa's Life Insurance

It may shock you to know that fewer than 2% of term policies will pay out. This is due to the fact that most people have an old school policy that ONLY provides a <u>death</u> benefit, not a <u>living</u> benefit. It may be time to bring your coverage out of the Stone Age and into the 21st century.

How likely are you in the next 20-30 years to experience cancer, a heart attack or a stroke, develop ALS, require a major organ failure, become disabled for a long period of time or any other number of tragedies? What if your life insurance policy covered more than death? That's putting the odds in your favor.

There are a handful of carriers on the market that offer these plans, often for a lower premium than regular life insurance.

Schedule a free consultation:

Looking For a New Career?

Maybe you recognize this "magic" formula for success:

1. Go to school, get good grades

2. Get a good job and work hard

3. The company will take care of you

And maybe you've discovered it's not all it's cracked up to be. Lucky for you, there is an insane amount of opportunity in our industry right now. And no, being an insurance agent isn't what you think.

In just a few weeks, you could be licensed and sitting in the driver's seat of your life as CEO of your own home-based business working around your schedule.

If you have a solid work ethic, love working with people, and are willing to learn, we'd love to meet.

You can fill out an application here:

What I will do as a result of reading this book...

ACTION ITEM

DATE

❏ _____ _____

❏ _____ _____

❏ _____ _____

❏ _____ _____

❏ _____ _____

❏ _____ _____

❏ _____ _____

❏ _____ _____

❏ _____ _____

❏ _____ _____

❏ _____ _____

❏ _____ _____

❏ _____ _____

❏ _____ _____

❏ _____ _____

❏ _____ _____

What I will do as a result of reading this book...

ACTION ITEM   DATE

❏ _____   _____

❏ _____   _____

❏ _____   _____

❏ _____   _____

❏ _____   _____

❏ _____   _____

❏ _____   _____

❏ _____   _____

❏ _____   _____

❏ _____   _____

❏ _____   _____

❏ _____   _____

❏ _____   _____

❏ _____   _____

❏ _____   _____

❏ _____   _____

What I will do as a result of reading this book...

ACTION ITEM   DATE

☐ _____   _____

☐ _____   _____

☐ _____   _____

☐ _____   _____

☐ _____   _____

☐ _____   _____

☐ _____   _____

☐ _____   _____

☐ _____   _____

☐ _____   _____

☐ _____   _____

☐ _____   _____

☐ _____   _____

☐ _____   _____

☐ _____   _____

☐ _____   _____

What I will do as a result of reading this book...

ACTION ITEM   DATE

❑ _____   _____

❑ _____   _____

❑ _____   _____

❑ _____   _____

❑ _____   _____

❑ _____   _____

❑ _____   _____

❑ _____   _____

❑ _____   _____

❑ _____   _____

❑ _____   _____

❑ _____   _____

❑ _____   _____

❑ _____   _____

❑ _____   _____

❑ _____   _____